FAITH

"This book is phenomenal and a "must-read" for all Christian parents who long for their kids to love the Lord with all their heart, soul, mind and strength. As parents of five children at different stages of development, this book provides needed insights for intentionally engaging each of them with the gospel."

—Dan and Micah Lindquist
Dan is the Managing Director of First Trust Advisors

"My only regret after finishing *Faith That Lasts* was that I hadn't read it before preaching a recent parenting series at my church. I would have recommended it as a super-helpful parenting resource for all the moms and dads in my congregation. Jon is a unique blend of parent, theologian, and pastor. Jon's advice to church leaders for reaching and discipling millennials is worth the price of the book."

—Jim Nicodem
Senior Pastor of Christ Community Church
Author of *Prayer Coach* and *Bible Savvy*

"I've known Jon Nielson since we were eighteen and freshmen in college. What I have seen in the years since is someone who loves the church because he loves Christ. Jon writes with clarity and crispness, walking the reader through the issues and the solutions. He writes with conviction and doesn't beat around the bush. And, as he has for all the years I've known him, he constantly points back to the real gospel as the solution."

—Barnabas Piper
Author of *The Pastor's Kid* and *Help My Unbelief*

"*Faith That Lasts* has something unique for young parents, older parents, grandparents, couples without children and church leaders. Each will benefit from the insights found in this book."

—Norm Sonju
Cofounder and former President & GM of Dallas Mavericks, NBA

"God loves children. Through his gospel, he creates fathers and mothers who love children. This is an incredible theological truth, but it takes a ton of wisdom to know how to enflesh it amidst the stresses and challenges of everyday life. In *Faith That Lasts*, Jon Nielson offers up a rich meal of just this wisdom—helping parents to own their God-given roles while encouraging us all to see that in the Christian home, love and truth, discipline and friendship, instruction and fun, do not conflict, but blend beautifully to the praise of our great God."

—Owen Strachan
Associate Professor of Christian Theology, Midwestern Seminary
Coauthor of *The Grand Design: Male and Female He Made Them*

"In *Faith That Lasts*, Jon Nielson guides us through the journey of parenting in a way that is biblically based, pastorally sensitive and practically helpful. As a parent, I'm grateful for being reminded of this biblical foundation. As a pastor, I'm excited for how this book will help churches play their role in the faith of young people and help young people play their role in the church."

—Jeremy Treat
Senior Pastor of Reality Church in Los Angeles

"To parents who are looking for encouragement to keep fighting for the faith of their kids, Jon Nielson offers a hopeful call to parents, millennials and the church to reaffirm our one true faith in the gospel of Jesus Christ—because it is here where parents will find what they need to fulfill their God-given calling."

—Brian Wildman, Executive Vice President at MB Financial
and Shelly Wildman, author, blogger and mother

FAITH THAT LASTS

FAITH THAT LASTS

RAISING KIDS THAT DON'T LEAVE THE CHURCH

JON NIELSON

CLC
PUBLICATIONS
Fort Washington, PA 19034

Faith That Lasts
Published by CLC Publications

U.S.A.
P.O. Box 1449, Fort Washington, PA 19034

UNITED KINGDOM
CLC International (UK)
Unit 5, Glendale Avenue, Sandycroft, Flintshire, CH5 2QP

ISBN (paperback): 978-1-61958-230-9
ISBN (e-book): 978-1-61958-231-6

Contents

PART ONE

1

Panic Attack

Surf around the Christian blogosphere often enough and before long you'll find the latest study about young people leaving the church. The reports vary, but they all seem to paint a very bleak picture.

- The Southern Baptist (SB) Convention found that eighty-eight percent of young people growing up in SB churches walk away from their faith.[1]
- LifeWay, 2007, found that seventy percent of "Christian" young people chuck their faith as adults.[2]
- A Barna study from 2006 identified that sixty-one percent of young people no longer attended church after their teenage years).[3]

What should Christian parents think? Is it time to panic?

Perhaps, yes—in a sense. Those of us who lead churches should be driven to our knees if even one young person who was taught the Word of the living God, proclaimed the one true Savior, lived out genuine Christian love, while caring for others with humility and grace says at the age of twenty-one, "No, I don't want that."

Why would a young person who has been brought up with faithful Bible teaching, and surrounded by genuine Christian fellowship and love, suddenly throw that all out the window?

Soul-Searching

No matter which percentage is correct, none of the recent studies on young people staying in church has been overwhelmingly positive.

Eighty-eight percent is bad; sixty-one percent is still pretty bad. Christian parents now, as always, should take time to do some soul-searching.

- What have we *failed* to teach our children in our homes?
- How have our churches *fallen short* of presenting and living out the true gospel of Jesus Christ?
- In what ways can young parents seek to *faithfully and effectively* pass on the gospel of Jesus Christ to their children so that they nurture a faith that lasts?

These questions have fueled the writing of this book. Almost every adult Christian knows someone who has been personally affected by the departure of a child from the church and the Christian faith as well.

For some of us, this hits very close to home. So many people are currently grieving and praying fervently for an adult son or daughter who no longer professes faith in Jesus Christ. Many reading this book are right in the middle of parenting and long to gain clear biblical principles that give guidance in raising children toward a Christian faith that "sticks." Those types of biblical principles are offered in this book.

Thinking Retroactively

I am not an expert on parenting. While we have three children of our own, my wife and I are still very much in the midst of Christian parenting with all of its struggles, frustrations and confusions.

Although we certainly pray and seek to guide them to Christ as best we can, it remains to be seen whether or not our children will give themselves earnestly to repentance of sin and a personal and genuine faith in the Lord Jesus Christ. I am no expert. I'm learning as I go, seeking to submit to God's Word at every step and often eagerly looking to the Christian parents around me for counsel.

Young people do not want anything fake and they absolutely despise anything resembling hypocrisy.

This book speaks from experience, research, interviews, anecdotal evidence and, most fundamentally, the truths of God's Word about some of the distinctive elements in Christian parenting that set some families apart. I have ten years of student ministry leadership behind me. I have taught, discipled, counseled, mentored and interacted with hundreds of Christian young people in the context of the local church. I have also seen many of these young people grow into adulthood, and have even married some of them. Many of them are still in our church, while others have relocated and are involved in other churches. Sadly, some young members have become statistics, having walked away from the church, and from Jesus Christ himself.

Here's what I have found helpful for both myself, and for parents around me: thinking *retroactively*.

In other words, we start with the "finished product," by looking back at what the parents did in a child's life that may have contributed to the present state of their child's faith in Christ and their involvement in the local church.

- We will look at those who have walked away from the faith, trying to see what their parents did (or failed to do) during their growing-up years.

- We will look at those who love Jesus as adults even more than they did as teenagers and try to see what their parents had in common as they raised and trained them.

Thinking retroactively means seeking to find some common traits (we'll call them principles) of young people who were raised in the church and grew up to embrace vibrant and joyful faith in the Lord Jesus Christ as well to serve His church during their adult years.

Room for the Holy Spirit

Let me say something right at the beginning of this book: Christian parenting is NOT a formula. Although we will be laying out what I believe to be biblical and effective principles in the coming chapters, these five principles are not a "guarantee" for raising "perfect" Christian kids. This isn't like a recipe—mix the ingredients together and you'll always get the same thing! Why is this the case? This is the case because the fundamental teaching of the Bible regarding the salvation of human souls is a miraculous work of God that takes place through the marvelous and powerful work of the Holy Spirit in the human heart.

The salvation of any person, regardless of background and upbringing, is a miracle. It doesn't matter where you were born or what kind of family you grew up in.

You and I were born into sin. We entered this world with blind eyes and a natural "bent" toward rebellion against God and disobedience of His commandments. All of us who are Christians, even those raised in godly Christian families, experienced a moment when God miraculously opened the eyes of our hearts to believe the gospel, discern the truth of Scripture, repent from sin and put faith in Jesus Christ as Lord and Savior.

Good parenting is certainly used by God because the life-giving gospel is often proclaimed to children through godly parents. It is God, though, who opens blind eyes and softens hard hearts. This is a work of the Holy Spirit, and this is precisely why Christian parenting must never be considered a formula.

On the (sad) flip side of this, some children are raised in godly Christian homes and grow up hearing the true gospel of Jesus Christ faithfully proclaimed to them, but they never believe it. They choose to reject the truth of God's Word and live as their own "gods," rather than submitting to Jesus Christ as Savior and Lord.

Although no parent is perfect, faithful Christian parents will need to stop placing blame on themselves at times and simply keep pleading with God to call wayward children to Himself by the power of His Holy Spirit. It's just not a formula; salvation is a miracle . . . for all of us!

Discerning Patterns

The purpose of this book is to discern patterns that I have observed in the lives and upbringing of young people who grew up in the church, stayed in the church, and went on to love Jesus and serve the church for many years.

We're not trying to find the parents who have done *everything* right! We are seeking to ask some basic questions and find some answers about what parents of young people with lasting and vibrant faith in Jesus Christ have in common.

Here are some of the questions that have led to this book:

- What do some parents do better than others that helps their children feel positively, rather than negatively, about church life, service and involvement?

- What characteristics can we identify in parents of Christian kids who have never gone through a "rebellious" period, or a time of great cynicism or disdain towards the church?

- What can we learn from Christian parents whose kids are even more vibrantly engaged with Jesus and His church in adulthood than during their high school years?

I'm answering these questions from both a pastoral and parenting perspective. I've watched young people grow up in our church, go to college, and walk away from the Christian faith completely. I've also watched people grow up in the same church, go to college, absolutely blossom in faith and witness for Christ and take leadership in churches around the world. I'm trying to get at what sets this second group of people apart from the first group, what patterns are distinct in them.

These patterns will serve to define the themes that will make up the bulk of this book. Again, these principles are not meant to be read as "promises" (i.e., do these five things, and your kid will love Jesus forever no matter what!). They are meant to serve as key foundation points for the way that we parents raise our kids to know and love Jesus Christ and to serve and love his church for a lifetime.

These adults spoke truth into their lives at many stages along the way.

Here are some of the basic principles we have come up with after several years of observations in student ministry in the local church:

- **Balance.** The parents who most often raise children who grow up to love Jesus and love the church are those parents who find a way, intentionally or unintentionally, to strike that right balance between "helicopter" parent and "do whatever you want" parent. In other words, these are the parents who are involved in their children's lives, but somehow avoid causing and exacerbating some of the frustrations (and often rebellion) that results from a meddling parent who is overbearing and controlling. These parents are usually especially adept at working gospel-centered and biblical conversations into the fabric of everyday life without seeming "preachy" and heavy-handed with their spiritual instruction. This balance will be discussed at length in chapter 3.

- **Modeling.** One trend that we are seeing more and more with every rising generation is the violent and fierce reaction from students toward anything or anyone that has even a hint of a lack of authenticity! Young people do not want anything fake, and they absolutely despise anything resembling hypocrisy. This is precisely why parents who preach a certain gospel but then live differently from that gospel in their home are often very much in danger of losing their kids to a rejection of the Christian faith.

  We will delve much more into this topic in chapter 4, but this can be seen in the contrast between a gentle and polite tone in public settings, contrasted with yelling and screaming in the context of the home. It can even show up in the cynicism that develops in the heart and mind of the young person toward a parent's "prayer voice," which only comes out in corporate worship! In contrast, the absolute best way to demonstrate the truth of the gospel to a young person is to seek to live authentically and consistently—in every setting and context of life. Sadly, far too many parents go through a serious shift—often without even realizing it, when they walk in the doors of their home after having been with their church friends.

- **Gospel.** The word "gospel," as central as it is to the Christian faith, can get over-used, especially with the return to gospel centrality in so many Christian circles in recent years! We cannot neglect to mention the important distinction between a home of "Christian morality" and a home that is truly formed around the "Christian gospel." Many homes, even homes run by parents who don't have a personal relationships with Jesus, seek to maintain themselves by living according to a basic set of Judeo-Christian values. Sadly, many Christian parents establish their homes on little more than these bare, naked values themselves.

  Of course, morality matters too! Christians are called to be holy followers of Jesus Christ who obey the Bible. What must not be missed, however, is the life-giving grace and power of the gospel of Jesus Christ that actually *empowers* obedience and holiness. Christian parents, in other words, are not just out to form "good" kids. They are after the participation in their reception, by faith, of Jesus Christ as Lord. Only through faith in Jesus Christ can young people be transformed by the indwelling power of the Holy Spirit and actually be equipped to obey the Word of God. Chapter 5 of this book will focus extensively on what a gospel-centered home should look like in contrast to a merely moralistic home.

- **Sharing.** "Sharing" in the context of this book will refer to the open-handed approach of Christian parents toward their children. In other words, the joyful sharing of their formation and teaching with other like-minded believers in the context of the church. Christian parents, according to my observations, whose kids have grown up loving Jesus and the church into their adult years benefitted from knowing lots of godly people of various ages and diverse backgrounds. These adults spoke truth into their lives at many stages along the way. The parents of these children didn't "cling" tightly to their kids, insisting that their voices be the only voices that they heard as they grew up.

On the contrary, they invited people into their kids' lives (godly people, of course!) who could partner with them in the overall purpose of discipleship of their children as followers of Jesus Christ. These are the parents who hold their kids loosely, entrusting them to God first and then to the wider body of the church second. We'll discuss what this can look like in chapter 6.

Our God and Savior loves our children more than we could ever hope to love.

- **Friendship.** Finally, the somewhat slippery issue that we'll try to wrap our minds around in chapter 7 is the all-important one of friendship with our children. After all, my observations have forced me to conclude that the kids who grew up with a healthy view of the church and a vibrant love for Jesus more often than not enjoyed a solid and healthy friendship with their parents.

It's not that the role of authority and leadership was removed; it's simply that these kids have grown up with parents with whom they have consistently heard this message (verbally or non-verbally): "I *like* you." Not just "I love you," but "I like being around you; I think you're fun!"

There is something about a fun-loving and joyful connection with our kids that lays the groundwork for deeply serious spiritual engagement, discussions, and even requests for advice and counsel as the years go on. The reality is that good Christian parents *do* find a way to be friends with their kids, even as they lead and discipline them when necessary, while preserving a role of leadership and authority.

Principles . . . Not Rules!

I will discuss this more in chapter 3, but what you will find here are not rules, but principles. These principles seek to expand and fill out the nature of a parent/child relationship that best enables genuine growth in Christ, and a lasting commitment to his church.

I will also address some ways churches in our country may better serve, engage with and equip the college and career-aged men and women in our midst. By God's grace, my prayer is that these principles and suggestions will be beneficial to Christian families and Christian churches, even as they continue to look to the Almighty God as the only One who can birth saving faith in the souls of sinful men and women of all ages.

Panic and Passivity

So, is it time for Christian parents everywhere to panic? No, not quite. In the next chapter, we'll discuss key points of evidence that actually show us that many young people who are genuinely *Christian* do indeed grow up to continue loving Jesus and actively participating in local churches. There is hope for Christian parents who commit their children to God's care and embrace some of the basic biblical principles that are put forward in this book.

However, not panicking is not the same thing as remaining passive. This book urges parents to put some time, sweat, and hard work into raising kids. These principles with which we'll engage are not just going to "happen." It will take work to get to know our kids, battle strains of hypocrisy in our lives, engage other Christians in our kids' lives and bring the truths of the gospel into the everyday lives of our families. This isn't easy stuff!

So, no, we don't have to panic when we see the latest statistics. But don't be passive either! This calling to be Christian parents is a weighty and God-given calling. It is not to be taken lightly! We need to work at this together—with our sweat, our prayers and our hearts.

The Power of God in Parenting

A friend of mine who is a new parent recently told me something that his father told him as parenting advice. His father said: "Son, it's really easy to be a bad parent . . . you just make the easiest choice in every situation!" My friend's father went on to say: "It's really, really, difficult to be a good parent." Isn't that true? Our sinfulness shows up in the way we're tempted to parent. It is almost always the easiest choice, with regard to our kids, that is the wrong one.

Don't discipline them; just let them off the hook.

Don't take the time to ask probing questions; just assume that everything is okay.

Don't say no when you know it's going to make them angry; just assume that it's okay just this once. See what I mean? We need to constantly fight the sinful tendency as parents to take the easy way out!

Friends, after reading and hopefully applying this book, let's take some time to commit to parenting prayerfully to God during these days. Let's ask the Savior to identify areas in our parenting styles and decisions that have not been earnestly and intentionally gospel-centered or biblically minded.

Let's plead with God to give us energy and joy, by the power of His Holy Spirit within us, to work, sweat and fight lovingly for the hearts and souls of our kids. Perhaps it's time for us to commit to working harder to know, love and disciple our kids!

For the "strivers," we also must not forget that we never engage in Christian parenting alone. Our God and Savior loves our children more than we could ever hope to love them. My wife and I constantly have to remind ourselves of this amazing fact!

As we work, sweat, teach, discipline and talk, my prayer is that the principles of this book point us consistently toward the God who alone can save the lost hearts of sinners. He saved us. He can grow miraculous saving faith within the hearts of our children as we faithfully bear witness to His Son. Remember that we are not raising our kids alone. Christ, the living Savior, is with us!

2

The Other Side of the Story

When most Christians hear some of the statistics that began the last chapter, we simply believe them. We take them without much consideration, skepticism or evaluation. "Well," we say, shaking our heads, "we must have a spiritual epidemic on our hands. We simply can't keep our kids in the church as they grow up."

And so, programmatic and structural changes become the immediate answer. Churches change musical style, lighting and venue. They may even change pastors! The goal is to become more relevant and better equipped to engage teenage members as they enter college and the career world. In writing this book, I've talked to dozens of pastors and church leaders who are borderline desperate because of the way youth in their churches seem to grow up and take off.

I'm going to ask a very simple question in this second chapter: Are young Christians really leaving the church? It's a complex question and every word in the phrase is important. Let me explain.

Are Young *Christians* Leaving the Church?

This is really a fundamental part of the question, and its answer will have tremendous implications for what the imagined solution might be for better reaching our young people. The question is this: Are genuine *Christians* growing up in churches and then walking away from faith completely during their college and career years?

Is something happening to young people at the age of eighteen that somehow reverses the amazing early work of the Holy Spirit in their hearts and lives and sends them into a tailspin of sin? If so, are local churches to be blamed for this? I first want to answer this question theologically. Then, I'll answer it practically and anecdotally.

A Theological Answer

Are young *Christians* constantly walking away from genuine faith (as opposed to the institution of the church) as they reach their late teens and early twenties? Theologically, the answer is "no," although, as we'll go on to consider together, they may be walking away from the institution of the church (temporarily, hopefully!).

The reason for this lies in the biblical doctrines surrounding our salvation, most importantly regeneration, conversion, justification and the indwelling of the Holy Spirit. Let me just take a moment to walk through each of these important doctrines.

Regeneration

The Bible makes it clear that apart from the miraculous work of the Holy Spirit to make an unbeliever "come alive" to faith and acceptance of Christ, no man, woman or child is capable of choosing Christ freely. Ephesians 2:1–3, in fact, tells a very sad story about our natural state apart from Christ.

> And you were dead in the trespasses and sins in which you once walked, following the course of this world, following the prince of the power of the air, the spirit that is now at work in the sons of disobedience— among whom we all once lived in the passions of our flesh, carrying out the desires of the body and the mind, and were by nature children of wrath, like the rest of mankind.

Paul goes on to discuss the way that genuine believers are made alive–raised with Christ to new life. The point is this: Dead slaves of Satan cannot choose Jesus Christ without the miraculous and regenerating work of the Holy Spirit in their hearts, making them come alive to be "born again" in faith, as Jesus explained to the Pharisee, Nicodemus, in John chapter 3. No church program can manufacture regeneration; it is the powerful, miraculous and mysterious work of the Holy Spirit acting on a sinner's heart as he or she hears the gospel of Jesus Christ taught, preached or explained.

Conversion

As the regenerating work of the Holy Spirit acts on a sinner's heart and soul, and repentance of sin and faith in Jesus Christ as Lord and Savior occurs, genuine conversion happens. That is, a sinner under God's wrath turns—perhaps drastically and intentionally—to become a repentant, humble and committed child of God and worshiper of the Lord Jesus Christ.

It's a 180 degree turn from service to self toward service to God. Yes, it's true that a conversion at age six can look a bit less drastic than an adult conversion after a lifetime of violence and drug abuse!

However, the miraculous change of heart is no less spiritually significant.

There are some young people who simply never genuinely repented of sin and trusted Jesus in a saving way.

A child born in sin and under God's wrath has entered the eternal kingdom of God through faith in His Son. The apostle Paul, in 2 Corinthians 5:17, puts it this way: "Therefore, if anyone is in Christ, he is a new creation. The old has passed away; behold, the new has come." This radical shift—with all of its newness—is just as drastic and significant in a child's conversion as in the conversion of a lifetime criminal.

Justification

As a man, woman or child responds in repentance and faith to the regenerating work of the Holy Spirit in his or her heart and is thereby converted, something else happens instantaneously.

According to the Bible, something that is radical, real, eternally significant, and even "legal," occurs: justification. When a sinner repents from sin and puts faith in Jesus Christ as Lord and Savior, the Bible teaches us that he or she is instantaneously forgiven and justified—made "right" with God eternally on the basis of the finished sacrifice of Jesus Christ on the cross for his or her sin.

Just listen to the amazing witness of Scripture to this point in Romans 5:1: "Therefore, since we have been justified by faith, we have peace with God through our Lord Jesus Christ." Justification means "peace with God." It's a peace that means total lack of conflict, in an eternal and lasting way, with the eternal and Holy Creator of all of us. He no longer holds our sins against us but has nailed them to the cross with His beloved Son. Justification, in other words, is permanent and unchangeable. It is God's doing, as a result of his Son's finished work on the cross.

Indwelling of the Holy Spirit

The Bible goes on to teach another amazing truth about those who are genuinely converted to Christ and justified by His finished and atoning substitutionary death on the cross: Christians are filled with the genuine presence of the Holy Spirit permanently.

Before conversion and justification, we all had no choice but to continue in sinful attitudes and selfish motivation; the Holy Spirit, after conversion, empowers us to live for God and to be more and more sanctified (made holy and set apart for God) each day.

The Bible makes an amazing statement about this directed at the Christians in ancient Corinth and also to genuine Christians today: "Or do you not know that your body is a temple of the Holy Spirit within you" (1 Cor. 6:19)? Christians are actually called "temples"—dwelling places for the very Holy Spirit, the third person of the Trinity. Again, this,

like justification, is not a reality that can just disappear. Jesus
sends forth the Holy Spirit to be His presence in the lives and
hearts of all who trust Him as Lord and Savior.

Now, what is the point of delving into these theological
terms and truths about regeneration, conversion, justification
and the indwelling of the Holy Spirit? The point is simple, and
yet profound: Salvation is God's work, not ours. Yes, human
beings respond to God in faith, and they often do so in a context or community of faith that presents the gospel clearly and
winsomely to them.

But, ultimately, the miracle of conversion and the security of salvation is God's work, not ours. You could actually
say (although I don't want to sound too crass) that if young
believers are chucking their faith at age eighteen, then something has gone wrong with God, rather than the church!

Because of these theological truths about the miraculous
nature of conversion, and the power of God in our salvation,
I wrote the following in the *Gospel Coalition* blog a few years
back about the importance of bringing back a focus on conversion in our approach to youth ministry in the context of the
local church.

> The apostle Paul, interestingly enough, doesn't use
> phrases like "nominal Christian" or "pretty good kid."
> The Bible doesn't seem to mess around with platitudes
> like: "Yeah, it's a shame he did that, but he's got a good
> heart." When we listen to the witness of Scripture,
> particularly on the topic of conversion, we find that
> there is very little wiggle room. Listen to these words:
> "Therefore, if anyone is in Christ, he is a new creation.
> The old has passed away; behold, the new has come"

(2 Cor. 5:17). We youth pastors need to get back to understanding salvation as what it really is—a miracle that comes from the glorious power of God through the working of the Holy Spirit. We need to stop talking about "good kids." We need to stop being pleased with attendance at youth group and fun retreats. We need to start getting on our knees and praying that the Holy Spirit will do miraculous saving work in the hearts of our students as the Word of God speaks to them. In short, we need to get back to a focus on conversion.

How many of us are preaching to "unconverted evangelicals"? Youth pastors, we need to preach, teach and talk—all the while praying fervently for the miraculous work of regeneration to occur in the hearts and souls of our students by the power of the Holy Spirit! When that happens—when the "old goes" and the "new comes"—it will not be "iffy." We will not be dealing with a group of "nominal Christians." We will be ready to teach, disciple and equip a generation of future church leaders— "new creations"!—who are hungry to know and speak God's Word. It is converted students who go on to love Jesus and to serve the church.[1]

So we see, ministry to young people in our churches is not about providing them with the perfect "package" of ministry and leadership that will be strong enough to last as they enter their college lives and careers in the real world.

The simple fact is that no matter how good our "package," it will never be strong enough to make an unconverted person say no to sin and yes to faith in Jesus Christ for a lifetime. We simply don't have the power to do what God alone can do in regeneration, conversion, justification, and the indwelling of the Holy Spirit.

Back to the question: "Are young *Christians* leaving the church and chucking their faith?" The simple, biblical and theological answer would be: NO.

Genuine Christians—those who have been regenerated by the Holy Spirit, converted through faith and repentance, and eternally justified on the basis of Christ's finished work on the cross and an indwelling by God the Holy Spirit—are not all of a sudden chucking their faith and turning to sinful attitudes and lifestyles.

The reason this isn't the case has very little to do with us, and everything to do with God. He has accomplished sinners' salvation, and He will bring it to its good end!

Before we seek to answer this question a bit more practically and anecdotally, let me just offer a couple of suggestions, in light of this theological discussion as to why young people do seem to "chuck" their faith during their college and career years.

They are never converted. Parents, you will hear me speak to this simple truth many times in this book. My prayer is that it will free you to trust God more and implore Him with your steady prayers for the children who have walked away from the church. Surely, there are many complex factors in each individual case, but ultimately, there is only one: a lack of genuine conversion.

Sometimes there are "warning signs" for what might come during the high school years; other times, students "walk the line" as long as they're under their parents' roof, biding their time and waiting to live in sin until freedom from rules and restrictions comes along. Whatever the case, here is the point:

A departure from the church and from faith in Jesus Christ during college or career years is not an *abandonment* of a faith once held dear; it is simply an *exposure* of what has never actually been a heartfelt and personal reality. Regenerate, converted, justified believers don't suddenly decide to throw Jesus away.

The Holy Spirit within them wouldn't allow it! Children who grow up in the church and walk away from the Christian community are simply beginning to live out a heart of sin and rebellion that was hidden for a period of years.

What does a person do when they attempt to take Jesus and throw away the church?

They are temporarily grieving the Holy Spirit. If the story of King David's sin with Bathsheba and Uriah recorded in 2 Samuel tells us anything; it's that even God's people are capable of terrible sins against God. David, called a "man after God's own heart," becomes guilty of deception, adultery, murder and a terrible abuse of power. It's a striking and horrifying account!

It is possible, then, for genuine Christians to engage in a time of sin and rebellion. We are all capable of great sin, as long as we live in a sinful world. Genuine Christians who engage in unrepentant sin for a time do so in direct conflict with the Holy Spirit of God that indwells them. They grieve God, their Father, in their sin.

Because of this, it seems biblically faithful to say that genuine Christians will turn back from such a period of sin toward repentance and faith—probably with great grief and tears!

This, I believe, is precisely what happened to King David when the prophet Nathan finally confronted him with those chilling words: You are the man! Psalm 51 is evidence of David's brokenness over his sin and genuine repentance, as the Holy Spirit within him did its work of conviction and sorrow over his rebellion.

It may be, friends, that your children are genuinely converted but have entered a season of rebellion and sin, grieving the Holy Spirit who indwells them. If this is the case, you can gently appeal to them and pray that God would awaken them to their sin by the power of His Word and Spirit.

Are Young Christians Leaving the Church?

In the previous section of this chapter my focus was on the word: "Christians." Are young Christians who are genuinely converted and justified followers of Jesus really chucking their faith suddenly as they reach age eighteen and go off to college? Theologically, the answer is "no."

Now, I want to try to answer this question a bit more practically and anecdotally, by focusing on another word: "church." Are young Christians leaving the *church*? That's a bit trickier. You see, it may be that the college and career folks are leaving *your* church, but are not walking away from the church generally. It can be even more complicated. Let's explore just a few of the trends, as well as explanations, for some of the departures that we know so well.

A Movement Away from Traditional Church

We need to begin by acknowledging that there is a trend today among twentysomethings who still claim to follow Jesus

Christ as Lord and Savior. Many of them have become disillusioned with the "traditional" church—moving away from
any formal involvement with churches, in favor of a kind of
spirituality that can be shaped on their own.

Here is how author and popular blogger Rachel Held
Evans describes what she sees as the frustrations from millennials about the traditional churches they grew up in.

> Despite having one foot in Generation X, I tend to
> identify most strongly with the attitudes and the ethos
> of the millennial generation, and because of this, I'm
> often asked to speak to my fellow evangelical leaders
> about why millennials are leaving the church. Armed
> with the latest surveys, along with personal testimonies
> from friends and readers, I explain how young adults
> perceive evangelical Christianity to be too political, too
> exclusive, old-fashioned, unconcerned with social jus-
> tice and hostile to lesbian, gay, bisexual and transgender
> people. I point to research that shows young evangeli-
> cals often feel they have to choose between their intel-
> lectual integrity and their faith, between science and
> Christianity, between compassion and holiness.[2]

So, the response has been, for many of these millennials, to
become disillusioned with church in general. Many of them
choose not to turn away from a relationship with Jesus; they
are rightly able to separate his teaching and sacrificial love
from the hypocrisy that they observe in the church.

Yet, they attempt to live out their faith independently from
any body of believers that would organize itself as a "formal"
church. "Give me Jesus; you can have the church" becomes
their mantra.

A prominent "spokesperson" for this movement is Bono—the lead singer of the pop band U2. Bono, a self-proclaimed follower of Jesus Christ, has publicly and openly distanced himself from the "organized" church for decades, accusing it of everything from hypocrisy to heresy, to systematic sin.[3]

Bono pursues wonderful social causes and has been open about his faith in the identity of Jesus as the Son of God. His failure to engage with God's people in a church, though, has become, for many millennials, the ideal picture of leading an independent life for Jesus without the messiness of life within the institutional church.

We must point followers of Jesus toward engagement with a local church, as imperfect and messy as that may become.

Let me suggest quite strongly that any movement toward embracing Jesus while rejecting the local church needs to be combatted with careful teaching and leadership.

The firm convictions of Christians of all ages must lead to loving attempts to bring followers of Jesus back to engagement with His body in all of its local manifestations of church bodies around the world.

To claim to love Jesus, without loving His self-proclaimed body is to spit in the face of a Savior who died to forgive and save individuals, and who also built His church! Here's how I put this information every year in my kick-off message on the church to the college students in our community.

Ephesians 1 describes the church this way:

> "And he put all things under his feet and gave him as head over all things to the church, which is his body, the fullness of him who fills all in all." (Eph. 1:22–23)

> The church is, over and over again, called the body of Christ. Jesus Christ is identified as the "head" of that body. Remember that last comment that I asked you to consider as we began this discussion? "I want to follow Jesus, but I don't want to be a part of a church."

> Take the imagery of the church as the "body" of Christ and Christ as the "head" of the church very literally as you interact with that comment. What does a person do when they attempt to take Jesus and throw away the church? They are—in essence—tearing apart the body of Jesus. They are decapitating him.

> What may have seemed at first to be an almost righteous-sounding statement becomes fiercely sinful and disrespectful, and it flies in the face of everything the Bible tells us about the relationship between Jesus and His church.[4]

There are, indeed, many young people leaving the church generally—walking away from engagement with God's people, while seeking to maintain an individual spirituality and relationship with Jesus on their own.

We must teach and plead against this trend. We must point followers of Jesus toward engagement with a local church, as imperfect and messy as that may become.

Life with Jesus means life in engagement with, and commitment to, His people.

Church Plants and Young Congregations

Now, we turn to a bit more positive alternative. Many young people may be leaving *your* church, but that doesn't mean they're leaving *the* church.

Here's what I mean: You will hear, probably, the sad news and statistics about churches closing its doors by the hundreds or even thousands each year.

Never mind that some of these may be from mainline denominations that have ceased preaching the biblical gospel; the numbers are still indeed startling. Sometimes even optimistic Christians who hope in God's good plan for the gospel can get discouraged, believing that the church is slowly dying here in America.

We would all do well to keep teaching the importance of engagement with the church.

But church planting in America is at an all-time high! According to one recent study, over four thousand churches are planted in our country each year, with that number steadily rising.[5]

With more and more churches considering church planting as part of their ministry, and even their responsibility, there are new gospel-proclaiming congregations being started up all of over the country each year.

The exciting part, and the way that this discussion relates to the topic of this chapter, is that many of these new church plants that begin each year are filled with a disproportionate number of men and women in their twenties and thirties. People in this stage of life are mobile, flexible and excited about new gospel projects—particularly in areas full of striking and obvious spiritual and practical needs.

Some men and women in their twenties and thirties may indeed be leaving our churches (many of them large, traditional, suburban and family-oriented), but they are headed to exciting new gospel church-planting works in places of great need and opportunity.

We should be praising God for this!

The recent emergence of *The Gospel Coalition* and *Together for the Gospel*,[6] two cross-denominational conferences and resource centers, have globally brought together Christians around the gospel. These organizations are both populated by a wonderfully young crowd of men and women involved in ministry.

There is a vibrant and committed generation of Christian men and women in their twenties and thirties preparing to step up and take the lead in our churches, in this country, in the years to come. Praise God for this!

All of this needs to be measured, of course, by a steady commitment to and pursuit of inter-generational ministry and church congregations. I am by no means advocating the departure of all young adults from established churches; that would be a disaster!

I'm simply seeking to stem the tide of the "panic" that sometimes grips those of us in established churches and to remind all of us that young Christians often move and become involved in newer gospel works, church plants and churches with slightly different stylistic approaches and dynamics.

Response from Churches

This discussion doesn't mean that churches should do nothing, especially if all the college and career folks *do* seem to be moving away from your church and heading to other places. Inter-generational churches are important, and every church should be making sure that twentysomethings are being engaged, included, trained and equipped for gospel ministry.

I encourage churches to engage with college-aged and early career men and women in significant ways. Create space for them to be trained and to use their gifts. Make sure we're mobilizing them and even bringing them into leadership roles as appropriate.

Later in this book, I'll spend time offering some suggestions as to how local churches can take significant steps toward connecting with the twentysomethings in their congregations more effectively.

Conclusion

When it comes to the local church, genuine Christians aren't going anywhere; God has "got that." As Scripture says, those whom God has justified, He will also sanctify and glorify (see Rom. 8:29–30); that work is squarely on the shoulders of the One who is far more powerful than us!

Some young Christians, though, may be moving out of our churches. This could be challenging if it means they are embracing a "churchless" Christianity. We would all do well to keep teaching the importance of engagement with the church, which is called in Scripture the very "body" of Jesus Christ.

The departure of young people from some churches can be just a part of God's greater Kingdom work through them, as they move to join and serve as part of gospel works that are moving forward in exciting ways.

Let's all commit to be mindful of this "big picture" of what God is doing in towns and cities other than our own.

3

Is That a Promise?

As soon as we begin discussions about the importance of good Christian parenting, it's almost a guarantee that one of the most often quoted verses about parenting will come up. You guessed it! Proverbs 22:6:

> Train up a child in the way he should go; even when he
> is old he will not depart from it.

It's a beautiful verse, one that captures the hopes and prayers of every parent who knows and loves the Lord Jesus Christ and wants the same for his or her children.

Proverbs 22:6 points to the value of Christian "training" in parenting; the value in pointing children to the way of God in word and deed. We trust that our children will continue to embrace and serve God as they grow older. This is, indeed, the picture of how Christian parenting and families are to look.

Promise or Principle?

The question becomes: Is this a sure promise, true in every situation? In other words, is this verse in Scripture telling me that, no matter what, if I raise my children in the Lord, directing them to the way of God, they will never "depart" from faith, the church or involvement with the people of God?

Conversely, we might wonder (if we have children who have walked away from the faith) if this verse implies that their departure means that we have not trained our children in the "way" rightly or sufficiently. How should we take this verse from Proverbs?

The answer lies in both an understanding of biblical genre and an understanding of the nature of humanity. First, let's look at biblical genre. The book of Proverbs belongs to the poetry and wisdom books of Scripture, along with Psalms, Song of Solomon, Job and Ecclesiastes.

Anyone who actually repents of sin and believes in Jesus is a miracle given by God!

While these books are every bit as much breathed out by God and inspired Christian Scripture as Genesis, Romans or the Gospel of John (see 2 Tim. 3:16), they do need to be read and applied in slightly different ways.

Generally, one consistent characteristic of the wisdom/poetry genre in Scripture is a starkly "black and white" view of the world. This contrast is demonstrated clearly in Psalms 1, which begins the Psalter and is probably a kind of "theme psalm" for the entire book, and perhaps for all of the wisdom literature! In Psalm 1, the "righteous" man is contrasted with the "wicked" man. There are only two ways to go, with no middle ground, and no room for compromise.

Part of the beauty and benefit of wisdom literature in the Bible is its clarity on the big issues of life; when it comes right down to it, there are really only two ways to live: for God, or against Him. Ambiguity, complexity and the "gray" areas are left to biblical narratives, where we often find tragically "mixed" characters who are nevertheless used by God and are part of His people.

Books belonging to wisdom and poetry literature in Scripture tend to make broad, general statements that are predominantly true but may not account for some of the complexities and anomalies of life. We could give countless examples of statements in Proverbs that are similarly *generally* true with a few exceptions.

Second, we need to understand the nature of humanity. If we gain any knowledge about men and women from the first few chapters of the Bible in Genesis, it's that mankind is hopelessly wicked and sinful, with a strong bent away from God and toward sin ever since the fall of Adam and Eve.

In other words, it is not "natural" for human beings to live in the "way" of God, no matter how much parents faithfully train us! Think back to our earlier discussion about God's miraculous role in human salvation. Anyone who actually repents of sin and believes in Jesus is a miracle given by God!

The first example of Proverbs 22:6 *not* being a hard and fast "rule" is the first family in the Bible. Adam and Eve were surely not perfect parents (none of us are!), and yet we can assume that they taught both of their sons, Cain and Abel, about their Creator, their sin and their need for obedience and faith. Two sons, raised by the same set of parents, with the same training, but two very different outcomes! Abel was a man of faith; Cain was a murderer, filled with the ugliness of envy, bitterness and sin.

Why is this discussion important? Because Christian parents need to understand the difference between the sure *promises* of God in the Bible, and the biblical *principles* that are set forth in, for example, the wisdom and poetry genre of the Bible.

God's promises—forgiveness through Jesus, heaven for those who trust him, the bodily return of Jesus to earth, the presence of the Holy Spirit with his people are unbreakable, unchangeable and true one hundred percent of the time.

God's principles for life on this earth, often revealed in places like Proverbs, are generally true for those who follow him. Consider Proverbs 15:1: "A soft answer turns away wrath, but a harsh word stirs up anger."

Does that mean that, in every situation, a soft answer will cause an angry person to stop being angry? No. But, generally, it is a wise instruction to God's people that a word of gentleness and restraint in a tense situation will quell the violent anger of a contentious person; this is the wise way for God's people to respond to anger.

In the same way, Proverbs 22:6 presents us with a general picture of how Christian parenting works. A faithful commitment to "training" our children in the way of the Lord will, generally, lead to a lasting commitment from them to Him, His people and His church.

Generally, this is indeed how it works! It doesn't mean that there are not exceptions; Cain, and the sinful nature of the human heart, proves that to us. Most of the remainder of this book will seek to "fill out" this principle, which is given to us in a foundational way in Proverbs 22:6 by showing what faithful training looks like.

Think of it not as rules that will always produce results, but general principles which should guide those who ultimately trust God, not themselves, for bringing about the salvation of their kids.

Getting Situated

Let's take a moment to get properly situated as we prepare to discuss the first principle of gospel-centered parenting in the next chapter.

Focus on Christian parenting that is geared toward a lasting faith in Jesus.

We began this book, in the first chapter, by considering some of the "panic" that is gripping the adult generations in the church today, as we continue to reel at the statistics rolling in about young people leaving the church as they grow older. We evaluated some of this, and we also considered some of the common responses from adult believers.

In the second chapter, we sought to measure that panic a bit, by looking first theologically, and then practically and anecdotally, at the issue of young Christians leaving the church and the faith.

Theologically, we noted that those who are truly converted do not just suddenly walk away from their faith (concluding that when young adults do walk away from faith and church, it can often mean that they were not genuinely converted).

Practically and anecdotally, we examined the growth of a "churchless Christianity."

This is a trend to be battled gently and firmly using teachings from God's Word to young Christians. We also considered the positive trend of church planting and the exponentially high numbers of young people who are involved in young church plants and gospel movements.

We are now ready to begin considering together some of the common characteristics that mark the young people who are converted, and grow up to love Jesus and continue vibrant service and ministry in the context of gospel-proclaiming local churches.

A Focus on Parenting

We've already established, theologically, that conversion is the miraculous work of the Holy Spirit in a person's life, bringing him or her to repentance of sin and faith in Jesus. We cannot forget the human perspective in this process as well. God, in his sovereignty and mercy, delights to use ordinary means all the time to accomplish his saving purposes in the lives of His people.

As we look at the storyline of the Bible, one of the major and most usual ways God brings people to faith in Him is through the generational witness to the truth of His Word, which occurs in family life. Here are a few examples of this beautiful plan of God revealed in Scripture:

- Moses, in Deuteronomy 6:7, calls the parents in the congregation of ancient Israel to be constantly teaching God's Word to their children, as the primary "voice" of biblical teaching in their lives. Listen to his instructions to Jewish parents thousands of years ago: "You shall teach them [the commands of God] diligently to your children, and shall talk of them when you sit in your house, and when you walk by the way, and when you lie down, and when you rise." Clearly, Moses understood that the main way that God's Word and truth would be taught and learned in the community of God would be through familial relationships.

- This is not just an Old Testament idea either! As the concept of "Israel" expands through the global salvation of Jesus Christ to include all who are the "true Israel," through faith in Him, the church becomes the primary place for inter-generational teaching, instruction and training in the truths of God's Word. Just listen, for example, to Paul's instructions to Christian fathers in the first century church at Ephesus: "Fathers, do not provoke your children to anger, but bring them up in the discipline and instruction of the Lord" (Eph. 6:4). Paul saw the parents' role of "bringing up" their children through teaching, discipline and to know God and serve Him as adults!

The focal question for the rest of this book will be this: *What is it that Christian parents can do, in the best and most powerful way, to raise their children to know, love and worship Jesus in a lasting way that is lived out in the local church?* We've established that parents can't manufacture conversion in the lives of their kids. But we've also seen that, biblically, parents are tasked with a huge responsibility in the lives of their kids.

Humanly speaking, we are the usual means used by God to lead children to a lasting faith in Him. Let's focus on Christian parenting that is geared toward a lasting faith in Jesus—a faith that keeps young people in the church into their early adulthood.

4

Principle 1: Creating A Delicate Balance

Caricatures of over-involved and obsessive parents can be quite humorous. We laugh at movies or television commercials that portray a grown man having his nose wiped by his mommy, or an over-the-top "daddy's girl" whose father buys her everything she wants (all she needs is to give that little pouting look!).

Similarly caricatured in parenting are those who follow the "hands off" approach to raising kids—letting them run wild all day. These parents allegedly have the "I want them to discover themselves in total freedom" kind of mentality.

If you're reading this book as a Christian parent, you certainly don't think of yourself as belonging to either of these extreme categories. No one sets out to be an obsessively over-involved parent. No one intends to be hands-off with his or her child to the point that discipline and instruction is completely ignored. Still, our personalities and tendencies as parents will generally lead us toward one of these two extremes. As followers of Jesus Christ seeking to raise our kids to know Him, it's good to expose our leanings for our good and for the good of our kids.

A Delicate Balance

Here are two brief personal examples from relationships I've had with families in this context.

I knew a young woman; let's call her "Emily." Emily was bright, kind, thoughtful and absolutely paralyzed by an excessively overbearing mother. Her mother hovered over her: getting involved in everything from homework assignments to dietary decisions to relationships with boys at school. It was over-the-top!

Not surprisingly, by the time Emily broke free from this "regime" and went off to college, the wheels quickly came off. She resorted to partying and living wildly, quickly casting off the burden of her well-meaning, but incredibly overbearing, mother.

Protection, though, can easily turn into an unhelpful "sheltering" and "smothering."

Another example of an extreme, "James," like Emily, was bright, creative, thoughtful and kind, but he happened to have a very distant and decidedly "hands-off" father. Because of this, James became known for seeking out, almost aggressively and in bothersome ways, relationships with older Christian men in the context of his church and school. He didn't seem to be able to engage with his own peers and classmates because he was constantly in search of a father figure.

James' story is not quite as tragic as Emily's, but there still seems to be some amount of unrest in his heart, partly because he had a father who remained quite spiritually unengaged with him.

Let's discuss the balance that is most needed between *overly involved* parenting (which can stifle, frustrate and sometimes exasperate children) and *under involved* parenting (which can, in its worst cases, neglect careful instruction and discipline). The Christian kids I observed, who grew up in the church and stayed devoted to Jesus and his people during their young adult years, had parents who enacted this wonderfully delicate balance of parenting.

This balance was an important factor in their growth. Almost all these "success stories" were neither stifled by their parents, nor ignored and completely left alone by them. To put it biblically, they have been "brought up" by their parents in the Lord—lovingly, carefully, delicately and firmly. Let's dive into this principle of balance a bit more.

The "Helicopter" Parent

The "helicopter" parent complex usually develops, and is eventually embraced, in incredibly subtle ways.

Almost always, the over-involved Christian parent begins with good intentions. Fathers who desperately want to guide and instruct their children to do things the right way watch their children's every move, correct them when they make mistakes and try to ensure success in all their endeavors.

Mothers have a God-given desire to protect and guard their children from the sinful aspects of our world and culture. They may monitor television viewing habits and guard their children from spending time with the wrong people in the wrong contexts. A desire to guide is good, and the conviction toward protecting children is God-given. Yet both of these tendencies can go too far as we saw in the "Emily" example earlier.

The "guiding" and "instructing" impulse, for example, can easily turn into "control." Again, this can be quite subtle; it involves the move from instruction and guidance to an overly manipulative and heavy-handed obsession with the child's every move.

Space for discovery, challenge or even mistakes is not created, and a child grows up with a hovering, controlling parent who won't allow him or her to learn from mistakes, because mistakes are never allowed to happen!

This can start from the earliest stages of life when a toddler is caught every time he or she is about to fall. The danger is that even a young child begins to get the idea that his or her actions don't really have consequences or effects; mom and dad control the environment completely.

The "protection" impulse, similarly, can subtly move toward intense over-protection. Of course, we as Christian parents are called to protect and guard our children from harm; please don't misread me on this!

As a father of three daughters, I am fiercely and passionately protective of them and would gladly give my life to defend them should God ever put me in a situation where that was necessary. Protection, though, can easily turn into an unhelpful "sheltering" and "smothering," which can be intensely damaging to a young and developing child.

In this kind of parenting relationship, the attitude toward children actually becomes driven by fear—a fear that they will be exposed to things that are sinful, dangerous or harmful. The impulse becomes, for parents, one that leads to a "vetting" of everything that comes toward our children—people, ideas and even some biblical concepts.

Dangers

You get the idea. We've described just two of the general impulses that can lead to an overprotective and controlling approach to Christian parenting (the "helicopter" parent). What are the dangers of erring toward this extreme in our parenting? What damage can be done when the delicate balance is upset in this direction?

Such a child faces the risk of never internalizing the gospel personally.

First, a child who has been "helicoptered" can often become almost "paralyzed" when it comes to making decisions and acting on his or her own. There is a tendency, from a child who has been controlled, to constantly look over his or her shoulder to check for mom and dad's approval and to seek their direction.

Sadly, we've seen several young people who were controlled and monitored, almost obsessively, by their parents during their growing up years, who are now paralyzed with inactivity and indecisiveness as young adults.

Not only are they anything but "self-starters" when it comes to church life and the pursuit of Christ, they have trouble making decisions about anything. Far too often, such young people end up staying very close to home and struggling to "strike out" on their own as bold, courageous and independent followers of Jesus Christ.

Another danger that comes out of this approach to parenting is that a child does not learn to think for himself or herself. There is a subtle distinction here from the point made above.

Not only do young people who have been "helicoptered" fail to act decisively and make decisions on their own, but they struggle to think and process issues in a way that is separate and distinct from their parents' voices—even as young adults.

Recently, my wife and I had a brief exchange with a young woman in her early twenties and her mother. We noticed an interesting dynamic: Every time we'd ask this young, twenty-one year old a question about her life, activities or relationships, she'd glance quickly over at her mother before she began to speak. Sometimes we noticed that her mother would actually "fill in" sentences for her daughter, interrupting her to make her answers more clear and full.

Here was a young woman, sadly, who had been so stifled by her mother that she was almost incapable of confidently holding an adult conversation about her life without referring to her mother for guidance!

It was such an extreme example of this unbalanced parenting approach that it left us feeling extremely awkward whenever we'd engage in conversations with the parent and child together.

Third, the danger of this extreme leaning in parenting is raising children who are "sheltered" to the point of being absolutely overwhelmed when they inevitably come into contact with unbiblical or sinful ideas, actions or agendas from the people around them. They are unclear about what to do.

Their growing up environment was so controlled that they have never actually encountered any of the ideologies and convictions that vehemently stand in opposition to the Christian worldview. Their parents have simply kept them from any contact. At best, they will be shocked when they finally do encounter people who think or act differently than followers of Jesus.

At worst, they will feel betrayed by their parents, and perhaps totally incapable of countering false beliefs and sinful behaviors on the basis of a personal, well-experienced, challenged relationship with, and commitment to, Jesus Christ. This leads to our troubling conclusion.

In my experience (which has been affirmed in conversations and interviews I've conducted), a child who grows up having been "spoon-fed," coddled and controlled—smothered by helicopter Christian parents—faces a very real and imminent spiritual danger.

Here's what that danger is: Such a child faces the risk of never internalizing the gospel personally and making real decisions and real actions based on internal conviction. This child has been acted upon, not called to act himself or herself in response to a living faith that is growing and flourishing personally in his or her heart and soul.

Our church practices both infant and believer baptisms, and I sometimes conduct a pre-baptism "interview" with younger children who are pursuing a believer's baptism. There have been a few times where parents have accompanied their young children to these interviews (which is fine).

It's troubling when, in such "interview" settings, the child has a hard time answering for himself or herself questions about a relationship with Jesus Christ, belief in the truths of Scripture and a conviction about his or her sin and need for forgiveness and salvation from God. Sometimes it's clear that the parent is driving the baptism, rather than it emerging from a real, deep and genuine conviction from the child.

My antennae are raised when a young person in such an interview context can define "the gospel" very clearly, but who balks at a follow-up question such as: "And how are you personally growing in Christ right now? What has God been teaching you lately?" Those kinds of questions often reveal the difference between a spoon-fed "head knowledge" and a genuine relationship with Jesus.

The majority of kids probably would never choose to eat vegetables and take showers, much less attend a corporate worship service every week!

Sometimes, if a child feels forced into "accepting" Jesus from a young age, he or she will pray a prayer just to make the parents happy, whether or not there is any personal belief or conviction. It's precisely *this* kind of manufactured spirituality that college-aged men and women tend to leave behind eventually; it was never theirs to begin with!

You've seen the first extreme, which can upset the "balance" in Christian parenting: the "helicopter" parent complex.

Whether through smothering, over-protection or obsessive and controlling impulses, this approach to parenting can actually do the exact opposite of what many Christian parents intend to do; it can drive children during their young adult years away from faith because it was forced on them—a faith that never had room to become theirs through careful thought, prayer and conviction.

The "Let It Go" Parent

Let's turn to the other extreme in parenting which can also upset the balance in a very different direction. This is probably one that most diligent and intentional Christian parents *don't* lean toward, but it should be described and acknowledged just the same. Unlike the "helicopter" parent approach, this approach—what I'm calling the "let it go" approach—gives children too little direction, guidance and intentional teaching regarding the gospel of Jesus Christ and the ways of God's Word.

You'll probably recognize some of these phrases and quotations, which you'll hear from these Christian parents sometimes.

- "We don't want to make him go to church because we want him to choose to go for himself."
- "She needs to make her own mistakes and find her own way."
- "My goal is to really be his friend; then he'll feel comfortable talking to me when he's going through a tough time."

Of course, there is a bit of wisdom in all of the sayings demonstrated here. We do, as discussed in the first part of this chapter, want our children to choose Jesus and His church because *they* see eternal value there and not just because we tell them to! We do want to allow our children enough space to learn from mistakes, rather than smothering them with control so that they are never able to see the effects of their actions.

We also want to nurture a relationship with our children that leaves doors open for open and honest conversation. (We'll talk much more about how to do this in a later chapter.)

However, when these sentiments are taken to an extreme, they can lead to a parenting style that is "hands off," to the point of actually neglecting the God-given call to raise, train, instruct, teach and guide our children in the ways of Our God and His Word. Let me describe this a bit further.

With regard to church, for example, we have seen some Christian parents take the utterly "hands off" approach, allowing their kids to make their own choices about whether or not they will attend corporate worship, youth group, church retreats or Sunday school.

The underlying sentiment is not always a bad one. ("I want *them* to want to go; I don't want them to go just because I'm making them go.")

The problem is that the majority of kids probably would never choose to eat vegetables and take showers, much less attend a corporate worship service every week!

Then, there's the "friend" approach to parenting motivated by a sentiment that goes something like this: "I want my child to feel like I'm her friend; I want her to be so comfortable with me that she feels like she can talk to me about anything."

We've seen examples of extreme forms of this in our context; you probably have, too.

The result is usually a relationship between parent and child that appears to be very fun and social; they're good "buddies" with each other. But, as we'll discuss in a moment, an over-emphasis on this can lead to a serious void in some important spiritual responsibilities in parenting.

One parent in our community took this to the extreme a few years back and actually decided it would be "cool" to buy alcohol for her teenage child and her friends.

Why not be the one there with them as they begin to experience drinking while underage? Needless to say, this (among other factors) served to send her child on a dangerous trajectory as she approached her college years.

Parents have a God-given role to be
intensely involved in the spiritual
development of their children.

Dangers

Sadly, the extreme "let it go" approach to parenting leads to some devastating spiritual results as well. It's a different set of dangers, of course, than the "helicopter" approach, but the dangers are there nonetheless.

Take the "let the kids decide whether they will go to church" perspective in this mode of parenting, for example. Although the desire for a child to "want it" on his or her own is right, the approach carries a dangerous potential toward a total failure in leading, guiding and training children in good practices and disciplines. That is our role as Christian parents!

Many times our children do not desire, on their own at a young age, to do things that we know are good for them. Yet, we make them eat vegetables and fruit. We make them take showers and brush their teeth. We do things like this, hoping and trusting that, one day, they will see the value that lies behind what we are temporarily forcing them to do.

The same is true of church involvement, as we say to our children: "This is what we do, because we love and worship God and value his people. As long as you are in our home, you will join us in church involvement. We are praying and hoping that you will come to treasure Christ and His people in the way that we do."

There's a danger accompanying the desire to just be "friends" with our kids so that they will feel comfortable with us. The danger here, of course, is that we become *only* a friend with about as much spiritual influence and authority as a peer! That certainly is an abandonment of being a parent, which includes being a teacher, guide, leader and foundation for discipline and instruction.

There's a danger here, too, because the "friendship" we've so carefully formed with our kids can get destroyed in a moment if there comes a time of needed confrontation or discipline. From a child who has been primarily "buddied up to" by the parent, the response can be: "Hey, I thought we were friends! What's with all the judgment?"

Ultimately, the danger to our children due to an extreme "let it go" approach to parenting is that we can potentially fail to embrace a very unique and God-given role as the spiritual authority in our children's lives, not merely a loving spiritual example. Let's turn once again to Scripture, as we try to navigate a balanced way forward and avoid both of these harmful extremes.

The Biblical Balance

Before we turn to the positive biblical vision for setting this "balance" in parenting, we need to take just a moment to work on understanding the tendencies—and perhaps idolatries—in us, which can lead to an "unbalanced" style of parenting in one of these two directions. This may be a bit of an uncomfortable exercise, but it's good for each of us as parents to know our weaknesses and temptations.

For the parent who leans toward the "helicopter" impulse, the internal spiritual danger that usually is lurking nearby is a failure to utterly trust the sovereign work of God in drawing children to himself by the power of his Holy Spirit.

Often, we want to give God a little "help" by seeking to dictate and form every detail of our children's lives in every way. In extreme cases, this tendency can give way to a full-blown problem with control, and perhaps even an idolization of our own directing of our children. The heart problem that lurks beneath an obsessive and controlling parent is often, sadly, this failure to trust God completely and his love for our children, even as we lovingly point them to him.

For the parent who tends more toward a "let it go" mentality, often a hands-off approach to parenting can be masking a deep resistance or hesitancy to totally embrace the God-given (and difficult) responsibility to train and "bring up" children in the Lord.

It's couched in good-sounding language, as we've discussed before ("I want them to want it for themselves"), but sadly, it can often cover up a lazy approach to parenting. Some of us need to be challenged to do the hard work of training, teaching and discipling our kids—as messy as that can be much of the time!

The Way Forward

As we now turn to Scripture, I suggest a balanced way forward in parenting—one that I have seen to be effective over and over, by God's grace, in raising up kids who embrace Jesus and stick with him into their early adult years.

There is no room for lazy and completely "hands-off" parenting from devoted Christians.

It's an approach that is formed carefully by paying attention to the *verbs* that the Bible uses to describe the call to Christian parents. Just read the following well-known "parenting" verses below, and pay attention to the verbs that are used (italics):

- "*Train* up a child in the way he should go; even when he is old he will not depart from it" (Prov. 22:6).
- "Fathers, do not provoke your children to anger, but *bring them up* in the discipline and instruction of the Lord" (Eph. 6:4).
- "Only take care, and keep your soul diligently, lest you forget the things that your eyes have seen, and lest they depart from your heart all the days of your life. *Make*

them known to your children and your children's children" (Deut. 4:9).

- "You shall *teach* them to your children, *talking* of them when you are sitting in your house, and when you are walking by the way, and when you lie down, and when you rise" (11:19).
- "The living, the living, he thanks you, as I do this day; the father *makes known* to the children your faithfulness" (Isa. 38:19).

What do you notice about the verbs that are used in these verses? Parents are commanded to "train" their children and to "bring them up" to know God. They are also, in many places in Scripture, commanded to teach God's Word to their children and to "make known" God's faithfulness and God's ways to them. There is strength to these verbs, but also a certain limit to them—there is a balance!

These verbs steer us away from a "helicopter" approach to parenting. The command to "teach" is much different than a command to "force." The command to "train" is different than a command to "control."

Christian parents are guided by God's Word to make known, with clarity and consistency, the truths about God and his salvation through his Son.

Children should never be in doubt about their parents' love for Jesus and conviction about the truth of his claims. Yet teaching and training is different than control, obsession and hovering. It's guidance, not domination.

For example, the Hebrew word for "train," in Proverbs 22:6, carries the sense of (in all of its other uses in the Old Testament) dedication.

That is, the training of our children is not a domineering and force-filled endeavor; it is actually very tied up with the way that we worshipfully "dedicate" them to God, for lives of service to him. The attitude is much more loving (like Hannah, mother of Samuel) than that of a drill sergeant or household master.

Second, these verbs steer us away from a "let it go" approach. According to the verses previously stated, parents have a God-given role to be intensely involved in the spiritual development of their children.

They are called to both "teach" *and* "train." There is no wiggle room here. There is no room for lazy and completely "hands off" parenting from devoted Christians.

While we are called to avoid control and obsessive "helicoptering," we are also clearly instructed by Scripture to make known clearly and consistently to our children the truths of God's Word; they are to be intentionally raised to know Him.

Conclusion

Here's where we are so far:

- Principle 1: "A Delicate Balance"
  Parents whose children grow up to love Jesus and remain active in the church tend to find the right balance between "helicopter" parent on the one side, and "let it go" parent on the other side. They are actively engaged in their children's lives spiritually, without falling prey to overly obsessive and controlling tendencies.

We already know that it's not always an easy line to walk. Yet the Bible calls us to live in this tension with the right balance between these two extremes.

Over and over again, I have seen this balance maintained carefully (of course not perfectly) by parents whose children grow up to know and love Jesus and serve the church. These children were guided, taught, and trained, but not dominated. By God's grace, they freely embraced and internalized the truths of the gospel that were clearly made known to them from an early age. May we maintain this "delicate balance" as we raise our kids in the Lord!

5

Principle 2: Modeling

If you talk to young adults who have decided to walk away from the church, there is a very good chance that, when asked, they will cite hypocrisy as one of the main reasons for their disillusionment. I've had many of these conversations, and you probably have, too! Here are some of the ways this sentiment is articulated by young adults:

- "The church is full of hypocrites—people who say one thing, and then act in a completely different way."
- "That church is so focused on truth; they have no idea how to be loving."
- "People at my church growing up were so judgmental; I finally just couldn't take it anymore."
- "I'm just sick of being with people who act like they have it all together on Sundays—dress up and look nice—and then live a totally different life during the week."

Delving into the hypocrisy of specific churches will not be my focus! Surely, there are churches full of both hypocrites and genuine believers who, while sinful, are living out their faith consistently and faithfully throughout the week.

The point I want to make is that even a perception of hypocrisy, or a "double life" that lacks authenticity and consistency between beliefs and actions, is a huge turn-off for young people who are growing up in the church. College-aged and early career folks can amaze me with their lack of perceptiveness about entertainment, pop culture, general biblical or theological knowledge and practical wisdom about daily life.

How can we model the Christian faith to our kids?

But there is one thing that young adults today are incredibly perceptive about: inauthenticity. Their "fake meter" is off the charts; they can pick out someone who is not genuine a mile away and it will turn them off from whatever that person is "pushing" faster than any other characteristic. If a church, pastor or community is perceived as "inauthentic," you've lost your young adults.

For example, I recently met with a young man who was turned off by (of all things) the dress of the pastors at a local church. They dressed in dark suits and ties every Sunday, which he interpreted as "business-like" and "professional." Was this an unfair judgment? Yes, of course. But, for this young man, the moment he thought he detected a lack of authenticity and a "business" approach to church worship, he was out the door.

Let's translate this dynamic to family life in a Christian home. If perceived inauthenticity or hypocrisy in a church community is a huge turn-off for young adults, then how much more so will a failure to be genuine destroy biblical training and witness in a family?

In an age when being "real" is embraced wholeheartedly by young adults, how unattractive will the Christian faith become to them if it is perceived as "fake" or as something that is "put on" on Sundays, and then taken off like a suit for the rest of the week at work and at home?

The focus of this chapter is on one simple word: *modeling*. Let's examine together the central importance of Christian parenting and carefully living out a vibrant Christian faith in the sight of our kids that is genuine, authentic and free from free-flowing hypocrisy.

This simple, but profound, principle of modeling has come up again and again in conversations with pastors, parents and young adults as one of the key ways that we help our young adult children avoid disillusionment with the church and with Christian faith.

The fact is this: A gospel faith that is joyfully and seriously embraced, and lived out by loving and faithful parents, is much harder to "chuck" than one that is perceived to be fake, inauthentic and sporadic.

One of the pastors I spoke with described parents whose children stay with the church into their adult years this way: "They are the same people whether they are gathering at the church or away from the church."

Our goal should be to commit afresh, as Christian parents, to live consistent Christian lives—personally and publicly—for God's sake, and for the sake of our children who watch us so carefully.

Biblical Foundations

The modeling I am proposing is tied to raising our kids to know Jesus and love the church into their young adult years. Yet, the starting point for a desire to serve and love Jesus with authenticity can't start with our kids; it must start with our own hearts!

Please hear me on this: Our pursuit of modeling the Christian faith for our kids can't be *first* about our kids; it must be first about our own love for Jesus Christ as Savior and Lord, for the good of our hearts and souls. This is something that can't be faked.

The book of James is a wonderful place to go in Scripture for calling out an apparent "faith" that is devoid of works of obedience, and how to live an entire life in accordance with what we profess. James famously declared this about the assumed separation that some people make between an assertion of the truths of Christianity and a life that is totally devoted to Jesus Christ in a genuine way.

> But someone will say, "You have faith and I have works." Show me your faith apart from your works, and I will show you my faith by my works. You believe that God is one; you do well. Even the demons believe— and shudder! Do you want to be shown, you foolish person, that faith apart from works is useless? Was not Abraham our father justified by works when he offered up his son Isaac on the altar? You see that faith was active along with his works, and faith was completed by his works; and the Scripture was fulfilled that says, "Abraham believed God, and it was counted to him as righteousness"—and he was called a friend of God.

> You see that a person is justified by works and not by faith alone. And in the same way was not also Rahab the prostitute justified by works when she received the messengers and sent them out by another way? For as the body apart from the spirit is dead, so also faith apart from works is dead. (James 2:18–26)

The first reason, friends, that we must seek to live out lives of genuine faith and obedience in the Lord Jesus Christ, consistently and wholly, has nothing to do with our children and everything to do with our hearts and souls.

The God who saves us by the blood of His Son calls us to total and complete obedience; to a complete transformation of thoughts, word and deeds for his glory and praise. This is anything but hypocritical; it involves seeking to worship Jesus with every corner of our lives!

But the Bible, in many places, also speaks to the power of a consistent and genuine godly life in bearing witness to the truth claims of Jesus and the gospel. Peter, for example, speaks to the early believers about the importance of consistently godly lives in relation to the watching world. Listen to his words.

> Beloved, I urge you as sojourners and exiles to abstain from the passions of the flesh, which wage war against your soul. Keep your conduct among the Gentiles honorable, so that when they speak against you as evildoers, they may see your good deeds and glorify God on the day of visitation. (1 Peter 2:11–12)

In context, Peter is speaking to those inside the church with a focus on the witness of their lives to those outside the church. The principle can absolutely apply to our children—especially during the years in which they observe our lives and come to an understanding of the gospel.

Peter evidently has the hope that the "conduct" of the Christians in ancient Asia Minor will serve to shut the mouths of those who would criticize their faith, and even lead them toward "glorifying" God with them as believers in Jesus.

Good deeds must always be accompanied by gospel proclamation, but they can help to show unbelievers (and, yes, even our unbelieving kids) lives that are being more and more transformed by a real gospel, a true Savior and a genuine faith in God.

"The best thing a father can do for his children is love their mother."

I vividly remember a young man who came to live with my family and me during my high school years. He had experienced a troubled childhood and was certainly engaging in what most Christians would consider to be a sinful and rebellious lifestyle. As a fifteen-year-old, I didn't quite know how to engage him with the gospel in winsome and conversational ways; I simply befriended him, and our family welcomed him into our home.

As the year went on, he became softened to the gospel message (he was attending church with us), and we later had the great joy of seeing him profess faith in Jesus Christ on Christmas Eve! He told me once that I was the "goodest" person he had ever met (his words!). In other words, the simplicity of the

Christian life, which my family and I had sought to demonstrate daily, had a huge impact on him as he watched us and also heard the Bible taught week after week.

Dangers Avoided

Before we discuss some very specific and practical ways in which we can model a consistent and genuine Christian faith to our children, let's discuss some of the dangers that this commitment to modeling can avoid. In other words, I want to examine some of the things that, given a parental model of genuine and authentic commitment to Jesus, kids will *not* be able to use as valid excuses to walk away from the church. Here are three examples:

1. *The gospel makes no difference in my parents' lives.*

By God's grace, our children should never be able to make this claim of us. This has nothing to do with perfection; in fact, if anyone sees our sins and our faults, it will be our kids! But with Jesus at the center of our lives, our words, our habits and our home lives, our children should *never* be able to grow up wondering if the gospel really does affect us in our everyday lives. They should see the marks of faith in Jesus on everything we do, especially in our response to our own shortcomings, sins, weaknesses and failures (more on this in a moment).

2. *My parents put on a good face at church, but they were totally different at home.*

A life of seeking to model a commitment to Jesus before the eyes of our watching kids should breed consistency of life, words, thoughts and deeds. There should not be a drastic "break" between who we are out in public (at church, with Christian friends, etc.) and who we are at home with just our spouses and our kids.

Again, perfection is not what is in view here; it's a consistency of character and commitment to Jesus that is not situational or dependent on who is watching. Your kids will absolutely be able to pick up from a very early age on "fake" behavior in public that bears no resemblance to what you're really like at home!

3. *My parents were all about rules and restrictions; that's all the Christian faith is really about.*

How many times have you heard this? I cringe every time I do! Of course, there needs to be rules in any Christian home. For Christians, there is a clear call in the Bible to obedience and holiness; this means rules and principles to guide our lives as we follow Jesus.

But a genuine *gospel* life that is modeled at home should never be able to be confused with legalism, cold moralism or strict rules without a foundation of grace. This excuse can sometimes be over-used by teens, of course, but often it does reveal a home life that has been only about rules and not about a Christ-centered foundation for obedience and holiness.

Pictures of Modeling

I want to offer some very practical and specific pictures of what modeling can look like for Christian parents as they raise their kids to know Jesus and love His church. These are some of the ways that we have seen parents, in our church context, live out their faith in Jesus "in front" of their kids.

These parents demonstrate with their lives everything they are affirming with their mouths to their children. So, how can we model the Christian faith to our kids and take some of the above excuses off the table for them?

Church Life

Perhaps the first way that Christian parents can model a genuine faith for their children is through a commitment to, and love for, the local church they attend. A love for the church is much more often "caught," than "taught"—especially during the early years!

In the same way, a cynicism about the church can be easily detected, even by young children. Parents' attitude toward God's people and the gathering of corporate worship is going to "rub off" on their kids from the very beginning stages of development.

The marital relationship must be engaged in with worship to Jesus and submission to God's Word.

One particular family from our church has managed to raise several children who all love being involved and serving in the local body of believers. Yet, the parents are anything but "pushy" with their kids.

The best way I can describe what has happened to their children, regarding their church involvement and service, is that the sheer enthusiasm and joy of their parents in engaging with God's people has "spilled over" into their lives and hearts.

The kids have grown up thinking that going to church, and serving in church, is *fun*.

Of course, this will involve teaching our children as well. We need to model church involvement (attending, serving, loving the people, etc.), as we also explain to our children why the church is such a priority in our lives as followers of Jesus Christ.

Jay Thomas, Pastor of Chapel Hill Bible Church in North Carolina, put it like this when I asked him for his thoughts on the issue.

> Families that have an ecclesiology usually generate children who have an ecclesiology! These kids believe in and behave according to the primacy of the local church. Even godly families, that do a lot of self-feeding on spiritual resources, but who do not have a strong theology and application of ecclesiology, will most likely generate under churched or consumeristic kids when it comes to church. Also, spiritually focused parents who themselves are very committed to a local church may not raise their kids with an ecclesiology.[1]

The families whose children we have seen stick with the church are, generally, from families with parents who actively, vibrantly, and intentionally love the church, and explain to their kids why they do.

Children in those families don't grow up with a separation between spirituality and church life (as Pastor Thomas describes above); they see their relationship with Christ as intricately woven together with life as part of His body—the local church.

Personal Devotions

Many Christian families have a time of family devotions which the parents establish in the home from an early age. Perhaps the Bible is read around the dinner table or Bible stories become a part of the "going to bed" routine. These are good things! Christian parents are wise to set aside time as a family to make God's Word prominent and a priority in the home.

But my focus on this specific point is the importance of Christian parents in modeling a personal, devotional commitment to the Lord Jesus Christ that is noticeable and obvious to their kids.

It may indeed be helpful and powerful for a father to read the Bible to the family after dinner; however, I would argue that it can be even more powerful—in the way of modeling for children—to wake up early in the morning to find their father bent over his Bible, or spending a few quiet minutes in prayer before beginning his day.

My wife grew up in a home where her dad modeled his faith. Her father was never involved in full-time ministry, but he would wake up day after day, sit in the same chair every morning and read his Bible and pray.

He didn't make much of it; there was no "look at me!" attitude accompanying this discipline. But, the example of making a priority of genuine and personal time with God was not lost on my wife and her three brothers. This relates to what we've said before about guarding against at least one excuse that our children might use to "chuck" a commitment to the Christian faith during their young adult years: "My parents didn't really believe this stuff anyway; it was just a Sunday thing."

We don't want them to be able to accuse us of having a faith that did not permeate our personal lives, our habits, routines and daily commitments. Additionally, reading the Bible and praying every day will be good for our hearts and souls, too!

Living out our faith means having the honesty and meekness to admit when we're wrong.

Marriage

I vividly remember the sign that my father had hanging by his side of the bed in my parents' bedroom in the house where I grew up.

In clear and bold letters, it read: "The best thing a father can do for his children is love their mother." He lived this out every day in his service to my mom, his attentiveness to her interests and concerns and even in the intensity with which he rebuked my brothers and me when we talked back to her or failed to show her respect. We knew my dad loved us, but we also knew that he cherished, cared for and defended our mother.

I praise God that I grew up in a home in which I never had to question my dad's loving commitment to my mom, or my mom's loving commitment to my dad. Their consistent and faithful love for each other was a given, a foundational pillar of our family, that was deeply connected to their faith in, and love for, Jesus.

I know that this is not the case for everyone, but God can redeem and heal children from broken families who have witnessed painful and damaging marital relationships and divorces.

However, in many Christian children's lives, the simple and clear witness of a loving marital relationship between their parents can be a compelling pull to gospel faith and life.

Think about it this way: As a parent who wants to model gospel faith and life to your children, your relationship with your spouse is the closest and most immediate relationship that is observed by your children almost every day.

The marital relationship must be engaged with worship to Jesus and submission to God's Word. What an opportunity to live out a gospel-centered relationship before the eyes of our watching kids!

Conversely, what an opportunity to damage our witnessing model for our kids if we treat our spouse with contempt, arrogance or a lack of kindness toward the person whom God has put closest to us on this earth.

For many of us, this point may call for a kind of spiritual "reset" on our mindset and approach to our marriage—for our own hearts, yes, but also for the sake of the "model" we are putting before our children.

When we speak kindly to our spouses and treat them with respect, we are showing our kids how to engage in human relationships with the love of Jesus at the forefront of our lives. When we lose our temper with our spouses or treat them with disrespect, we can be in danger of implicitly telling our children that the gospel may be true . . . but it doesn't touch the relationships that are closest to us in the day to day.

Humility and Repentance

Just the other day, while I was working on something in a separate room from my two oldest daughters, an "altercation" between them had begun. I acted quickly, assumed that my oldest daughter was at fault and disciplined her for what had happened.

As the whole "story" unfolded, I realized that I had acted wrongly; the altercation wasn't her fault at all, and I had acted rashly.

Humbled by my mistake, and feeling badly for my daughter, I bent down, looked her in the eye and apologized and asked forgiveness from my four-year-old little girl. Good news: She forgave her imperfect dad!

This category of modeling may be the most difficult for all Christian parents because this has to do with our own willingness to *be* Christians "in front of" our children—with the humility, repentance and brokenness that it often demands.

Living out our faith means having the honesty and meekness to admit when we're wrong, to explain our sinful tendencies and even ask for their forgiveness when we make mistakes. Pastor Tom Olson, Campus Pastor at The Orchard Evangelical Free Church in Illinois, explains.

> "Certainly, the largest majority of kids who have stayed faithful to Christ come from homes where the parents have given them a faithful gospel witness since birth and who are humble, grateful believers in Jesus Christ themselves. That genuine humility and gratitude rooted in the gospel is vital. The students I've seen struggle the most with Christianity are homes that are practically

legalistic or where the kids think their parents faith isn't genuine—just a show or routine."[2]

As Tom Olson mentions, the children who grow up thinking their parents faith is just a "show or routine" are often the ones whose parents have never allowed them to see humility, brokenness, repentance or any kind of genuine struggle in faith or growth in Christ. They've put on a "perfect" aura, with the appearance that everything is put together all the time and nothing is ever amiss in their spirituality or their behavior.

This is a high calling; none of us will be perfect in the application of these principles.

Many times this can come from good intentions. We want to be good examples to our children; we don't want them to see our sin and mistakes, because we want them to imitate our good behavior. I get this!

But how will our children learn to humbly admit mistakes unless we model that for them, too? How will our children embrace a steadily growing faith in Jesus and love for him, unless they see us steadily and honestly trying to grow in our Savior? How will our children learn to forgive those closest to them when they are wronged, unless we give them the opportunity to forgive us when we make mistakes?

Sometimes the most powerful way for Christian parents to model the gospel to our children is to say (when we have made mistakes, lost our temper, treated them unfairly, etc.): "I'm so sorry. I was wrong to act in that way. Will you forgive me?" In our experience, it's harder for children to become cynical toward that kind of honest and humble faith than toward one that maintains the illusion of never making a mistake.

Evangelism

My cousins used to get embarrassed by their dad because no matter where he was, he would find a way to talk to people about Jesus. They have stories of conversations with gas station attendants, hotel clerks, car repairmen and cleaning ladies—all recipients of a warm and winsome gospel proclamation from their father as my cousins looked on, feeling slightly awkward. However, years later, they're immensely grateful for their father's passion for evangelism.

This final point can be the most difficult by far—especially for those of us who don't feel especially gifted as "evangelists." Even Christian parents who are extreme introverts can commit to being ready to bear witness to Jesus with people they know and meet, in a way that demonstrates a commitment to a courageous gospel witness for their kids to see.

What message does it send to our children when we go to church on Sunday, read the Bible around the dinner table but then never actually talk about Jesus and the gospel when we're "out" in the world?

What does it convey when we never mention Jesus in conversations, social gatherings or daily interactions with friends and acquaintances? Will they not begin to see Christianity as, at best, a personal and private matter and, at worst, something that we're slightly ashamed of?

When we speak to people, particularly unbelievers about Jesus and the gospel, we are implicitly telling our watching children that we are not ashamed of our Savior.

We are declaring to them as we model gospel witness for them that the salvation that Jesus Christ offers is the most beautiful, important and glorious part of who we are and the greatest gift we can offer to our friends, co-workers, relatives and even strangers!

We are modeling for them an entire life that lives, breathes and bears witness to Jesus Christ as Savior and Lord. They might get embarrassed by us, but they won't be able to call us fake!

Conclusion

We've come to the end of our second principle in gospel-centered parenting. Here's where we are so far:

- Principle 1: "A Delicate Balance"
  Parents whose children grow up to love Jesus and remain active in the church tend to find the right balance between "helicopter" parent on the one side and "let it go" parents on the other side. They are actively engaged in their children's lives spiritually, without falling prey to overly obsessive and controlling tendencies.

- Principle 2: "Modeling"
  Parents whose children grow up to love Jesus and remain active in the church tend to model well a genuine faith to their children through their own love for and service to the church, humility and authentic faith and love for spouses and people around them. They "practice what they preach," so that their kids cannot accuse them of hypocrisy.

This is a high calling; none of us will be perfect in the application of these principles. Yet, each one of us, as Christian parents, can seek to earnestly and intentionally pursue Christ in every area of life—for the eternal good of our own soul, and for the good of our observing children.

6

Principle 3: Sharing the True Gospel

Just the other night, in a gathering at our home, I asked a group of twentysomethings to share with me some of the reasons their peers give them for no longer being interested in Christianity or the church. Their answers were sad, although I can't say they were incredibly surprising. Here are the typical responses:

> "I have a friend who says she's done with the church because it's just about rules. She's no longer interested in a bunch of legalistic restrictions on her life."

> "Most of the people I know are tired of 'church people' who seem to be out of touch with reality; the truths they preach don't have anything to do with my real life."

> "For me, the Bible is just too hard to understand, and it's too difficult to try to relate to a God I can't see through an ancient book that's hard to read."[1]

I'm sure that many of us can probably add to that list from our own experiences with young adults. Here is the interesting realization I've come to as I've now had dozens and dozens of these kinds of conversations with college and career folks: *almost never do I find a young man or woman who has understood and grasped the true biblical gospel, and the person of Jesus Christ, and rejected THAT as legalistic, irrelevant, or boring.*

In other words, it is almost always a false substitute for the true biblical gospel that is rejected, rather than the true gospel and the person of Jesus Christ.

It's this simple fact that leads us to the focus of this chapter: There is a great need for the true biblical gospel of Jesus Christ to permeate the parenting of our children.

Far too often, it is another "gospel" that we are actually preaching; our kids are not rejecting Jesus, but the substitute for him that we are pushing on them. We need to ensure that the true, life-giving gospel of Jesus Christ is the foundation for everything we do in parenting.

What Is the Gospel?

There are some "go-to" passages in scripture that help us summarize the biblical gospel clearly and succinctly, and we'll look at several of these in just a moment.

First, we need to begin by being clear that the word "gospel" means "good news." This is fundamentally important!

The biblical gospel is not a religious system, a set of rules or even a call to obedience (although a right reception of the gospel will certainly lead to obedience). First and foremost, the gospel is "good news" for sinners. It is a joyful declaration of what God, in Christ, has done. Let's look at some of the key passages on this important topic.

> Paul, a servant of Christ Jesus, called to be an apostle, set apart for the gospel of God, which he promised beforehand through his prophets in the holy Scriptures, concerning his Son, who was descended from David according to the flesh and was declared to be the Son of God in power according to the Spirit of holiness by his resurrection from the dead, Jesus Christ our Lord. (Rom. 1: 1–4)

In the beginning of Paul's letter to the Romans—the letter in which he most fully develops, explains and applies the gospel—he summarizes what the gospel is fundamentally about. The gospel is about Jesus ("concerning his Son"), who is both human ("descended from David") and fully God ("declared to be the Son of God in power").

This was God's good plan for us from the very beginning of time.

What Jesus accomplishes in his death and resurrection is, according to Paul, "promised beforehand" in the Scriptures. The entire Old Testament looks forward to the gospel that Jesus will bring!

> Now I would remind you, brothers, of the gospel I preached to you, which you received, in which you stand, and by which you are being saved, if you hold fast to the word I preached to you—unless you believed in vain. For I delivered to you as of first importance what I also received: that Christ died for our sins in accordance with the Scriptures, that he was buried, that

> he was raised on the third day in accordance with the
> Scriptures. (1 Cor. 15:1–4)

Paul, in his letter to the ancient church at Corinth, identifies the gospel as the message of "first importance"—the gospel was the fundamental teaching that he delivered to these early Christians! He summarizes it with three main points.

First, Christ died for our sins (the sacrificial and substitutionary death of Jesus).

Second, Christ was buried and then raised (the real resurrection from the dead of Jesus, which guarantees eternal life for all who believe in him).

Third, this salvation from Jesus was "according to the Scriptures" (God's plan from the very beginning, witnessed by the prophets and by God himself throughout history).

> But now the righteousness of God has been manifested
> apart from the law, although the Law and the Prophets
> bear witness to it—the righteousness of God through
> faith in Jesus Christ for all who believe. For there is
> no distinction: for all have sinned and fall short of the
> glory of God, and are justified by his grace as a gift,
> through the redemption that is in Christ Jesus, whom
> God put forward as a propitiation by his blood, to be
> received by faith. This was to show God's righteousness, because in his divine forbearance he had passed
> over former sins. It was to show his righteousness at the
> present time, so that he might be just and the justifier
> of the one who has faith in Jesus. (Rom. 3:21–26)

These few short verses are packed with depth and meaning as Paul summarizes the gospel of Jesus Christ again in the letter to the Romans. The key points here are that what happens through Jesus' death on the cross is an absolute fulfillment of God's perfect justice (human sin is really paid for) and God's grace towards sinners (we can really be fully forgiven). Paul uses three key words to help us understand what Jesus' death on the cross does.

It offers *justification* for us; we can be "declared righteous" before God. It offers *redemption* to us; we can be "bought back" from slavery to sin and death. It offers *propitiation* for us; we can truly be freed from God's wrath against our sin, because Jesus drains the cup of God's wrath in our place and removes it from us.

Many more passages in Scripture explain and apply this central message of good news. These are just a few beautiful summaries that all Christians should have in their "back pockets," because they help explain the gospel clearly. The following can be considered to be the key elements of the message of "good news" that is proclaimed to us in the Bible:

- Jesus is fully God and fully human, and he died on the cross in the place of God's people.
- Jesus' death offers sinners real forgiveness, salvation and peace with God.
- Jesus' resurrection secures salvation, giving hope for eternal life for all who believe in him.
- Jesus' death and resurrection has been God's plan for salvation from the very beginning.

This gospel is, indeed, the "good news" that the Bible declares to us. God, the Creator of the universe, has not left us to die in our sins. He has come near to us, through his own Son, who died in our place and rose again to give us eternal life. This was God's good plan for us from the very beginning of time, and it's now been declared to us as something we can receive by faith.

This is the biblical gospel of Jesus Christ—good news of salvation from sin, which can be accepted by any man or woman as a gift from God!

Non-Gospel Parenting Models

Having identified the biblical gospel, let's identify some of the problems with "non-gospel" parenting models. These models are absolutely not centered on the good news of Jesus' death for sin, resurrection from the dead and the life of faith that can be lived in Him. Here are just a few examples:

A Moralistic Model

I remember a conversation with a parent whose teenage child was struggling with rebellious behavior and sinful choices. We talked for fifteen to twenty minutes, and I allowed the parent to share his frustration with the child's behavior, as well as his hopes for change.

After a substantial amount of time, I began to realize that not once had this parent mentioned the heart of his child, or anything related to faith in Jesus, the gospel or the grace-driven approach to obedience.

It was very difficult to discern whether or not this parent wanted his child to know and love Jesus, or just learn to behave in a way that would be less embarrassing and socially unacceptable. It is painfully obvious that many Christian families substitute a vague sense of moralism for a thoroughly gospel-centered approach to parenting and family life. Moralism refers to the governance of a certain set of morals such as be nice, be honest, be kind, etc. that are the ruling features of a home.

These general moral commitments are referred to constantly by parents while children are called to live up to them (e.g., "Sarah, you need to be nice;" "We don't interrupt in this family;" "We always tell the truth"). Many times these moral commitments are thoroughly grounded in and emerging from a relationship with Jesus and a commitment to him, at least for the parents.

Even the spiritual aspects of raising kids becomes a pragmatic way to achieve that goal.

However, in a moralistic model, only the morals themselves are transferred to the children; they hear instructions and the "moral code" for the family, but they fail to understand the way these morals are meant to be the fruit of a vibrant relationship with the Son of God, who died for sinners to give them new life.

Although morals in themselves are not bad, they have no power. Moralism will ultimately prove ineffective in raising children of faith if they are disconnected from the person and work of Jesus Christ.

A Legalistic Model

Legalism can be closely connected to moralism, as described above. Yet, there's a more precise definition for legalism.

In legalism, men and women are embracing a rules-based approach to earning favor either with God, or with fellow human beings. It's a "legal" system based on adhering to strict rules and the accrual of merit based on keeping the rules.

Most Christian parents who believe the Bible will certainly not teach their children that they can earn God's favor and be saved by keeping all the rules of the Bible carefully and perfectly.

Hopefully, there's an understanding of the grace and mercy of the cross somewhere in there! But often the relationships and standards that are established for the home can implicitly teach a legalistic understanding of the Christian faith. This can happen in at least two ways.

First, some Christian parents can focus almost primarily on the "rules" of the home, without any explanation of the "heart" behind the rules.

I'm not implying that every time we punish our kids we need to go through the whole gospel narrative in order to understand the basis for obedience and holiness; however, if they never understand *why* we maintain rules in our homes, they'll struggle to have a bigger understanding that is not legalism.

Second, some Christian parents can unwittingly allow their relational warmth with their children to be directly correlated with their kids' behavior. They treat their children in a different way *relationally* after they have broken the rules. I'm not talking about punishment; that needs to happen.

But, if the tenor of the relationship changes after our children have disobeyed, we can be in danger of implying to them that our love toward them is based only on their keeping the rules. That can "fly in the face" of what we want to show them about the unconditional love of God toward his children and subtly build into them a legalistic understanding of Christianity (keep the rules, and God will be happy with you; break them, and you'll feel him frowning at you).

That's simply not the biblical understanding of what it looks like to be children of God who are justified, forgiven and totally at peace with a loving Father through faith in Christ.

A Theocentric (not Christocentric) Model

This approach is a step in the right direction, away from moralism and legalism, because this parenting model has God as its focus. Parents using this model do a good job of grounding the "house rules" in the person of God, saying things like: "In this house, we obey God in all we do," or "God comes first, then family, then work and school and sports."

Children grow up in this context with a sense of God as a divine presence, distantly overseeing their lives and impacting their moral decisions and behaviors.

The problem here is that purely God-centered parenting can miss the central fact of the New Testament—that God has revealed himself perfectly and finally in the person of His Son, Jesus Christ (see the beginning of Hebrews 1).

Theocentricity without Christocentricity doesn't give kids the whole story; it doesn't allow them to clearly put together how their God and Creator is just, and also merciful and gracious. Theocentricity doesn't confront them daily with the reality of being able to relate to their holy God through a loving Son who has made a relationship with God possible for them. A "God-focused" family can sometimes be in danger of using God simply as a kind of "figurehead" floating over everything, but never someone to connect with personally and intimately.

A Pragmatic Model

Finally, there is what I'll call the "pragmatic" model of parenting. This one is tricky to pick out, because sometimes it can even make use of Christian language, and even a Christ-centered focus. Here's the catch in this model of parenting: There is some *other* ultimate goal that parents have for their kids—something different from loving and worshiping Jesus and being utterly devoted to Him.

Gospel-centered parenting is marked by Jesus during the "along the way" moments of life.

It's the goal of achieving success, good behavior, popularity, etc. that becomes the controlling focus of parenting. Even the spiritual aspects of raising kids becomes a pragmatic way to achieve that goal.

In this case, Jesus' name can be used to help kids be more moral; church can be just another method to get children who are well-connected and well-behaved. In the pragmatic approach to parenting, the gospel may be part of it, but it's a tactic toward some other goal, rather than the goal itself.

Implications of a Gospel-centered Model of Parenting

These are some of the alternative models of parenting that are not explicitly grounded in the biblical gospel. Sadly, even parents who grasp the biblical gospel—the good news of Jesus' death for sinners and resurrection from the dead sometimes do not let that amazing good news permeate their parenting in the way that it should.

Some of these parents find themselves reverting to a moralistic or pragmatic model; they're unwittingly giving their children only some of the implications of the gospel, rather than the objective beautiful foundation of the gospel.

As gospel-centered parents, we need to make sure that we're starting our kids at the cross of Jesus Christ and moving outward from there.

But what does this actually look like? What are some ways, practically, that we can begin moving toward a parenting model that is grounded in the biblical good news of Jesus Christ?

Getting Practical

What is offered here is not a comprehensive description of a "gospel-centered parenting" model; there have been others who have done that. There are many biblically solid and theologically rich guides written by godly and thoughtful men and women, which would serve as wonderful resources!

What is discussed here is a few sketches of what gospel-centered parenting begins to look like, in contrast to the models identified earlier, which fall short of this gospel model.

Deuteronomy 6—"Along the Way"

In Deuteronomy 6, Moses, in the midst of his "sermon" on the Law of God, makes some remarks to parents within the community of Israel. His remarks have huge implications for the way that we speak truths about the biblical gospel into our

children's lives. Re-read these often heard words from Moses
to God's people.

> Hear, O Israel: The Lord our God, the Lord is one.
> You shall love the Lord your God with all your heart
> and with all your soul and with all your might. And
> these words that I command you today shall be on your
> heart. You shall teach them diligently to your children,
> and shall talk of them when you sit in your house, and
> when you walk by the way, and when you lie down, and
> when you rise. You shall bind them as a sign on your
> hand, and they shall be as frontlets between your eyes.
> You shall write them on the doorposts of your house
> and on your gates. (Deut. 6:4–9)

The picture that Moses paints of the teaching and training
of Christian children in the ways of God is not a lecture that
occurs once a day around the dinner table. It is not a once-a-
week family attendance at the church service. It is an *ongo-
ing conversation* about the things of God that permeates every
part of life continually.

Christian parents are called to talk about God's grace and
mercy "along the way"—in the midst of daily routine and
activities. They are called to be naturally speaking about the
cross of Jesus in the midst of morning preparations and eve-
ning clean-up.

Gospel-centered parenting is not a system, but a way of life.
My parents served me extremely well in this regard. It was a
rare occasion that my dad or mom sat me down for a "formal"
time of teaching. And yet, every struggle, difficult situation
or agonizing decision that I faced with their help was—from

their end—permeated by gospel truth because that was simply what "oozed" out of them.

In other words, as gospel people, they could not help but allow the truths of the biblical gospel to "leak" into the details and conversations of everyday life.

One kitchen conversation in particular is burned into my mind. It began as a dating talk; I casually filled them in on some details about the young woman with whom I'd been spending time lately.

The need to submit to the authority of the parents appropriately comes first for most kids.

As they shared insights, struggles and mistakes from their past, they also pointed me to the beauty of a Christ-centered marriage. That little conversation had a lot to do with setting my trajectory for good desires in relationships, dating and, eventually, Christian marriage.

I remain convinced that as our children see the way that we naturally speak about and apply the biblical gospel "along the way," as Moses describes, they will begin to see more and more of its power, reality and influence on everyday life.

After all, the truths of Scripture and the salvation of our Lord Jesus are meant to infuse every moment of our lives with meaning and purpose. By God's grace, we can begin showing this to our kids when we walk, when we drive, when we wake up, when we go to bed, when we rejoice and even when we grieve. Gospel-centered parenting is marked by Jesus during the "along-the-way" moments of life.

Forgiveness

I recently heard a devastating account of a man, who is now old, whose parents withheld affection and attention from him when he was not acting in the way they wanted him to act. By his account, they would literally ignore him, sometimes for days at a time, when he had acted out in some way. Then they would shower him with praise after he had done something perfectly in accordance with their wishes.

God himself must change
our children's hearts.

What a grace-less situation in which to grow up! Even today, this young man still struggles with a challenging lack of confidence, as well as a near inability to accept the good news of God's unchanging and amazing grace and love toward him in Jesus Christ.

The simple power of offering forgiveness to our children is a way that our parenting can become more and more marked by the gospel of Jesus Christ—the gospel of the Lord who has so richly and deeply and fully forgiven us through his death on the cross.

Far too many parents discipline when wrong has been done and offer praise when obedience is performed without any deeper explanation—to even young children—about what is really going on.

I'm convinced that even my young children are beginning to understand the need to not merely be disciplined and "put back in line" when they've disobeyed, but to actually be forgiven. They can sense when they have offended me or their mother by not obeying our words. They know there has been wrong and hurt done, and that this is wrong.

In fact, my four-year-old, as she's learned about forgiveness at church and in books, has even begun to ask me quickly after disobeying me: "Daddy, do you forgive me?" Of course, my assurance of full forgiveness, love and restoration is always quickly offered.

When we offer forgiveness to our children, we are giving them a picture of the gospel and teaching them about how we are living out the implications of the cross of Jesus Christ. This is even more true when we explain this to them gently and powerfully, with the biblical language of sin, Christ's forgiveness to us and the need for God's grace.

Our interactions with our children can become potential times of teaching about their sinfulness and their need for God's grace, which is much bigger and more perfect than ours! Listen to how Pastor Eric McKiddie put it when I invited him to comment on some of the characteristics of young people who grow up to love Jesus and believe the gospel.

> *They grasped that they were sinners who need grace.* Some students participated frequently in youth events and were basically good kids, but you couldn't tell if Christ was dear to them. Then there were those who were clinging to the cross, depending on God's undeserved love every day, because they knew they were sinful before his eyes, apart from Christ. Even as I think back to my own friends from my youth group days, I can see this being a huge factor between those who kept following Christ and those who drifted away.[2]

How does a child begin to get to the point described above by Pastor McKiddie? How does a boy or girl begin to come to a conscience admission of his or her sinfulness, as well as a joyful embrace of God's undeserved love toward them in Christ? It surely starts with a model of forgiveness and grace that is extended to them by parents who hold them accountable but who also explain to them that their unconditional love is grounded in the love of God toward them in Christ.

Calls to Obedience

Some of us get very nervous in the midst of a discussion about gospel-centered parenting, with its focus on grace, forgiveness and unconditional love. It's not that we believe those things aren't true or important, but we also don't want to minimize the centrality of discipline and the serious calls to obedience and holiness in Scripture.

I, in fact, do think it's possible to over-emphasize, or at least over-apply, "grace-centered parenting" as central as the concept of grace is to the Bible and the biblical gospel. I want to affirm the importance of discipline, instruction and authoritative calls to obedience for our children as Christian parents.

But I want to call us to the gospel foundation, which must always ground these calls to obedience expected from our children.

When kids are very young, Christian parents do need to often establish a simple, God-ordained order into reality in the home and family: Mom and Dad are in charge, and children are not.

The need to submit to the authority of the parents appropriately comes first for most kids—before any deeper "gospel understanding" of how their obedience fits into a response to God's grace to them in Christ!

The work of conversion, after all, is work that only God can truly do.

But as children get older, it is the duty of gospel-centered parents to help them understand more and more how obedience—submission to parents, holiness in actions, care with words and treatment of other people—is all grounded in their response to the God who has shown them grace and mercy in the cross of his Son.

We can all be more intentional about grounding our calls to obedience in the gospel of Jesus Christ—not in an "earning" method of salvation or a "just be a good kid" kind of moralism. Consider, just for example, your treatment of a child (who has professed faith in Christ) after a serious sin or lapse in judgment.

Both the moralistic model of parenting and the gospel-centered model of parenting are going to demand punishment; a confrontation, rebuke and the disciplining of a child for behavior that is sinful and disobedient. But, the moralistic model will leave the child going away saying: "My parents want me to *be* better. I've got to try to do a better job." The gospel-centered model will, by God's grace, direct the child toward a higher reality and a grace-grounded call to obedience.

We want our children to go away saying: "My parents took my sin and disobedience so seriously because of the seriousness of Christ's death for me on the cross. They reminded me that God's grace has been poured out in my life; I'm called to live in obedience to him."

We want to be giving our kids the true biblical gospel.

One parent in our congregation, for example, is always careful to tell his children that his discipline toward them happens *because* he loves them. Because he loves them, he submits to God in disciplining them and helping them learn to obey.

He explains, over and over, that his end goal for them is to love and obey Jesus because they want to . . . not out of fear of discipline and punishment.

In short, he makes every case of discipline into an opportunity to share the gospel with his kids!

This is a process, and no Christian parent does it perfectly. Still, the principle remains: Calls to obedience are gospel-centered when they are grounded in the gospel.

We are called to "do" in light of what has been "done" for us, in Christ. This simple fact can change the way that our kids receive our discipline and rebukes when they sin.

Prayer for Conversion

This last "sketch" of gospel-centered parenting should actually probably come first and should stand by itself as the most important one of all! Most fundamentally, and most basically, a gospel-centered approach to parenting involves prayerfully petitioning God to do His amazing and miraculous work in the hearts of our children. The work of conversion, after all, is work that only God can truly do.

If every one of our children is under God's wrath (Rom 1:18), dead in his or her sins (Eph. 2:1), and desperately fallen short of God's glory and goodness (Rom 3:23), then the problem is much bigger and more desperate than the solution of any parenting model. God himself must change our children's hearts, leading them to repentance of sin and saving faith in Jesus Christ.

We have a group of parents in our church congregation who have been praying together for almost ten years for their children, many of whom are now out of college. Some of the children are walking with the Lord; others are not.

This group diligently and consistently meets together to join hands in lifting their kids up to the Lord in prayer. It's a great model to young couples in our church of fervent prayer for the hearts and souls of our children.

A Diagnostic

And so, yes, we do all of these things. We want to speak the gospel clearly to our children "along the way," forgive them, demonstrate grace and reject lesser models of moralism and legalism. But, after all, it will not be our methods that bring them into the eternal kingdom of the Lord Jesus Christ; it will only be the miraculous work of the Holy Spirit, making them come alive to faith in God and love for his Son.

Let's consider this: Are we praying fervently for our child, or just worrying about him or her? Are we petitioning God to do His mighty and miraculous saving work in our child's heart, or merely hoping that he or she stays on a good and respectable path? Our prayers, after all, will reflect our hearts' deep desires for our children.

[Parents] seek to infuse daily life with gospel truth.

Let's make them "gospel" prayers—ones that petition the throne of God for the work of his Holy Spirit in their lives, which alone can awaken them spiritually and give them saving faith in Jesus.

We've only begun to scratch the surface of gospel-centered parenting; there is so much more that could be said. If you're wondering whether or not the parenting of your children is being properly infused by gospel centrality rather than some lesser principle, you might begin by asking yourself these diagnostic questions:

- Do I tend to focus *only* on behavior with my children, without actively and intentionally explaining to them a Christ-centered foundation for that behavior?

- Am I consistently showing unconditional love to my children, even when I need to discipline and punish them for disobedience? Do I say "I forgive you" to my children and then talk to them about God's forgiveness of us in Christ?

- Do I pray actively and consistently for the genuine conversion of my children, by the work of God's Holy Spirit in their lives and hearts?

- Am I explicitly directing my children to faith in Jesus, not just respect for God generally?

- Is my end goal—my greatest desire for my children—that they know, love and worship the Lord Jesus Christ? Or do I have some other hope for them that practically overshadows this?

I would encourage you to move through that list slowly and prayerfully in the next few days. Ask God to give you strength and discernment to continually evaluate your own parenting. We want to be giving our kids the true biblical gospel, which is grounded in the person and work of the Lord Jesus Christ. After all, there's no power in any other "good news" than that!

Conclusion

So, we've come to the end of our third principle in gospel-centered parenting. Here's where we are so far:

- Principle 1: "A Delicate Balance"
  Parents whose children grow up to love Jesus and remain active in the church tend to find the right balance between "helicopter" parent on the one side, and "let it go" parent on the other side. They are actively engaged in their children's lives spiritually, without falling prey to overly obsessive and controlling tendencies.

- Principle 2: "Modeling"
  Parents whose children grow up to love Jesus and remain active in the church tend to model well a genuine faith to their children through their own love for and service to the church, humility and authentic faith and love for spouses and people around them. They "practice what they preach" so that their kids cannot accuse them of hypocrisy.

- Principle 3: "Gospel"

  Parents whose children grow up to love Jesus and remain active in the church tend to be ones who have established a gospel-centered approach to parenting, rather than an approach that is purely moralistic, legalistic, pragmatic or even only theocentric. They seek to infuse daily life with gospel truth, directing their children to, not a religious system, but the person and work of Jesus Christ (death for sins and resurrection from the dead), who alone gives power for obedience, faith, and holiness.

Next we'll take a look at how Christian parents can intentionally work to include others in this process, as we discover Principle 4: "Sharing."

7

Principle 4: Sharing

In an article I once wrote in partnership with The Gospel Coalition, I made the following statements about the primacy of parents in the evangelism and discipleship of their children.

> Parents must be willing to prayerfully, humbly and yet boldly take responsibility for the spiritual growth of their children, as much as it depends on them. I don't mean to heap blame on faithful Christian parents whose children have turned away from Christ despite their best efforts to speak the truth of the gospel into their lives and live as godly examples to them. Rather, I want to challenge parents who perhaps fail to feel the full weight of their responsibility for praying, teaching, sweating and even weeping for the sake of their children's eternal destiny.
>
> Parents must commit themselves to the *evangelism* of their kids—seeing themselves as the primary "missionaries" in their lives. This involves a commitment

to speaking verbally, clearly and often the truth of the gospel of Jesus Christ and all of its implications. It means actively and intentionally making the Bible the central voice in the home, reading it to the family and explaining it as clearly as possible. Parents must commit themselves, also, to the *discipleship* of their kids. This activity moves into the area of relationship and application. It is involving our children in our lives, pursuing a genuine relationship and teaching them with words and example how to actively apply the truths of the gospel in everyday life. Christian parents, do you view your home as the first wave of evangelistic and discipleship ministry in the lives of your children?

Second, parents should never presume that the church will do the work that is primarily theirs. Relying on a youth pastor or church mentor to serve as the primary gospel-shaping force in the lives of our children will actually almost guarantee the *failure* in that task for even the most gifted and godly youth leader. How can a youth pastor realistically encourage a high school boy to read and study the Bible if that boy has never seen his Christian father doing the same? In the context of the local church, the effective youth pastor seeking gospel growth in the lives of students *reinforces, strengthens and bolsters* a gospel work that has sprung out of—and been nourished already within—the context of a Christ-centered home.[1]

As you can see, I've got some pretty strong convictions about the central importance and role of parents in the spiritual lives of their children. I think the biblical model for passing along the faith from generation to generation is grounded in families—fathers and mothers telling their kids about God, and the church being continually built up through the evangelization of the younger generations.

Invite other believers into the lives of [our] children as they grow up into faith.

Fathers and mothers who surrender willingly their responsibility to evangelize and disciple their children are failing to embrace a God-given call. Gospel training and discipleship begins in the Christian home; this is how God has designed it to work!

And, yet, this is not what this chapter is about. (Although, you might argue that this is what the last three chapters have been about.) I want to speak primarily to parents who are already convinced of what I've just stated, and everything that I quoted from that.

Here's what I mean: There are many Christian parents who are absolutely convinced that the primary role in the discipleship and training of their children belongs to them, and they take that role extremely seriously. They take it so seriously, in fact, that it can almost become an obsessive and *possessive* force in their lives.

They fail to fully and freely invite other Christians into the lives of their children. Christians who are God-given members of the body of Christ are meant to be partnering with them in the training and teaching of their kids. In very extreme cases of this, children grow up only hearing the voice of their parents, without the loving and relational reinforcement of the church community and the involvement of mentors who are not related to them.

That leads us to Principle 4 in parenting: "Sharing." Let's examine what it will look like for Christian parents to actively, purposefully and intentionally "share" the raising of their kids with the church community God has given to them.

It is important (and a God-given purpose) to invite other believers into the lives of our children as they grow up into faith. This characteristic—"sharing"—is central to the commitment of Christian parents whose kids tend to embrace both Jesus and His people in their young adult years.

The Other End of the Spectrum

I must first take a moment to acknowledge that some parents' tendency will be toward "sharing" in extreme ways! These are the parents who, perhaps because of failure in the discipleship of their children, or simply because of the rebellion and disobedience of their teenagers, adopt a kind of "you fix them!" mentality toward their children's youth pastors, mentors or teachers.

The attitude is one of throwing up their hands in the air, hoping that someone else will be able to engage their kids spiritually in ways that they have not been able to.

When I served as a high school pastor several years ago, I had several phone calls and meetings with parents who had, perhaps unwittingly, stepped into this "extreme sharing" zone. They approached me, not for partnership, but for a complete hand-off.

Now, of course, their language was not quite this extreme; they'd say: "Could you just meet with Brian, and see if you can help him." That, on the surface, is not a problem; of course I was willing to meet with Brian . . . that was part of my job as a youth pastor! But the more we would talk, the more it would become clear that the parent was "done" with regard to spiritually pursuing his child.

The parent was not saying: "Help me engage my son; let's do this together!" The message was loud and clear: "I don't know how to do this; please do it for me. Fix him . . . please!"

**It might be time to make a new investment
in the lives of other families in the church.**

Parents who find themselves in this mindset need to be gently called out—by pastors and church leaders—to a prayerful and intentional spiritual engagement with their rebellious or obstinate children. They need to be lovingly reminded that this ministry and witness is not just for the "experts" (youth pastors, counselors, etc.), but for parents who love Jesus and desperately love their kids.

It doesn't take a PhD, but it does take intentionality, engagement, loving conversation, patience and perhaps some early mornings or late nights in conversation and prayer. It's never time to give up on our kids spiritually and completely hand them off to someone else!

Resistance to Sharing

But then there is the other side of the spectrum—parents who would never "hand off" their kids to someone else and who, in fact, resist even allowing too much influence from other people, even Christians, in the lives of their children. Why might this be?

First, it could come from some very good intentions. Many Christian parents have a desire for their children to hear a consistent message—one that is true to Scripture, faithful to gospel-centered teaching and tied to their specific theological convictions.

They are confident in their own ability to deliver that message and that gospel training to their children, knowing that they have forged a relationship with them and have learned how to speak to them in a way that they can understand.

**Consider finding some other
like-minded parents and families
with whom you can connect regularly.**

Such parents are deeply committed to their children; they are not intimidated at all by the high call they have as Christian parents and tend to hold that call very tightly.

Second, though, there may also be a problem that comes from a certain idolatry of *control*. For some Christian parents, the one factor that gives them hope and security with regard to their children's spiritual development is the closeness and intimacy of their involvement with every decision, life experience, struggle and interaction of their kids.

In other words, their confidence in God's work in the lives of their children is very tied to *their involvement* in the lives of their children. This can become an idol—something that is worshiped, valued and used as a way to bring a feeling of significance and security.

Parents suffering from this idolatry can fall prey to habits that turn into addictions, as they obsess over controlling every detail of their children's lives. When you have an obsession with control, you're not going to invite other Christians into the lives of your children; that would involve surrendering control.

Third, we need to acknowledge here that, for some Christian parents, a general distrust and disillusionment with youth ministry has contributed to a reticence toward sharing discipleship of children with other Christian people.

As a former youth pastor, I will be the first to admit that some of this reticence has been well earned by the youth ministry community!

Far too often, youth ministry has been full of significant problems, most notably: an obsession with what is "fun" and "cool," rather than what is theologically and biblically substantive; a separation, rather than a deep connection, with the local church body and inter-generational worship and community; a focus on numbers, rather than a focus on intentional training and discipleship toward relationships with Christ that lasts into young adult years.

It's certainly not wrong for Christian parents to identify these problems in youth ministry and to react by wanting to pull their kids closer toward them in discipleship, training and teaching.

Sometimes, though, the reaction has been far too extreme, as parents develop a distrust for, not only youth ministry, but the influence of any younger Christian adults in the lives of their kids. This leads to the final reason for resistance.

Some resistance to "sharing" the discipleship of our children with other Christians in the church can come from a deep fear of rejection by our kids. It is quite easy to become uncomfortable with our children developing close mentoring/discipleship relationships with Christians who are older than them and yet quite a bit younger than us.

Again, there is probably some warrant for worry here; it has been the sad habit of some "cool" youth ministry leaders to pit children against their parents, setting themselves up as the ones who really understand, listen and "get" where the kids are coming from.

This is a devastating mistake for a youth leader to make; it goes against what I believe is the core goal of youth ministry, which should be a joyful partnership with Christian parents in the teaching and training of Christian kids!

Consider encouraging your children to find
a place in the church where they can be
involved and serve *independently from you.*

It's this mistake that I believe has led many parents to resist opening their kids up to significant influence and mentoring from youth pastors, leaders and ministry workers.

They simply don't want to have to compete with someone whom they suspect might try to make them into the villains; they don't want to be rejected by their kids in favor of a young, cooler spiritual influence.

These are just a few of the reasons Christian parents can sometimes resist the "sharing" of their children with other believers in the church. If we're honest, we can probably see a bit of ourselves in all of these; we all have, as parents, insecurities and idols that we need to battle prayerfully by the power of the Holy Spirit. It's helpful to identify our tendencies, as we continue to seek the ultimate and eternal spiritual good of our kids.

So, how do we move forward in this "sharing"—the fourth principle of godly parenting that can lead to faith that "sticks" into young adult years?

Sharing: How Do We Do it?

Allow me to offer a few examples of how this commitment to "sharing" can look in the lives of Christian parents and children. As you read these, consider the ways that you can joyfully open your arms to the involvement of others in the lives of your children—for their eternal good!

Church Involvement

The first and most fundamental sphere for this "sharing" of the discipleship of our children is the context of the local church. Now, we've discussed already (in the "modeling" chapter) the importance of Christian parents leading the way in church attendance, involvement and ministry.

Here, I want to focus on how to engage in church life in a way that intentionally "shares" our kids with other believers in our community. What can this look like?

It might look like engaging with other families in the church in a more intentional and relational way. If church has become, for you, merely a place of once-a-week attendance, rather than a focal point of ministry, service, discipleship and relationship, it might be time to make a new investment in the lives of other families in the church. Consider finding some other like-minded parents and families with whom you can connect regularly—at church and outside of church—for the sake of your kids.

As a child, I was deeply marked by the faith of my parents, but I was encouraged by the faith—and the different personalities and insights—of my friends' parents as we spent time in their homes and had meals and times of fellowship with them. As my parents opened up our family in relationship to the other families of the church, they exposed me to other parents and children who loved Jesus, but who sometimes did things differently.

Sometimes I learned new insights or behaviors; other times, I actually became more convinced of the wisdom of some of the ways my parents chose to do things! Consider "opening" your family up to other families in your church and intentionally walking through life together as you work to raise godly children.

You might also consider taking steps to serve together, as a family in the context of the church in situations that involve many other believers. We have families in our church, for example, who serve together in the disabilities ministry each week.

This gives them an opportunity to have a common goal and cause in ministry, but it also enables the children to connect with other believers with whom they serve and work.

As a family, they are together becoming part of something that is bigger than just their family unit, as they join together in partnership with other believers. Other families have engaged on a short-term mission trip together along with several other families who have children.

Again, here is an opportunity to open up our kids to the influence of other Christian families, who may be able to encourage and challenge them in ways that we may not even know they need!

Let me add, too, that some Christian parents might need to begin to allow their kids to find their own way in the context of the church with regard to their specific "place" of engagement, ministry and service. When every interaction and engagement with the church is tightly controlled, the process of engaging with the church as a unique part of the body can be hindered and slowed at times.

The younger years are times to invite other believers into their lives to provide help in mentoring and discipleship.

Consider encouraging your children to find a place in the church where they can be involved and serve *independently from you.* During the younger years, perhaps this is in the context of children's ministry or the nursery.

As they approach high school years, maybe there are ministry opportunities with older people in the congregation, outreach events or short-term mission trips.

I am convinced that it is probably never too soon to begin gently pushing our kids toward engagement with Christ's church in their own specific ways, which employ their own unique gifts, passions and abilities.

Allow them some space to figure this out, and watch them begin to identify their place in the body of Christ. You might have to be willing to admit that their place is different than yours! After all, according to Paul's metaphor, they may be "feet," and you may be "hands" (see 1 Cor. 12).

Youth Ministry

Much could be written here (and much has been written!) about the hot topic of youth ministry and the failure of certain youth ministry models. There are also some solid biblical models available for youth ministry moving forward.[2] But, youth ministry itself is not the focus of this part of the chapter.

I want to encourage Christian parents toward utilizing youth ministry in the right ways, as it can contribute to the "sharing" of discipleship and training of their children.

First, though, I will briefly summarize my convictions regarding the proper place of youth ministry in the local church; I do believe that it can, and should, be done well.

A few years back, I wrote about the proper place of youth ministry in the local church.

> A church-focused youth ministry has leaders who go out of their way to remind the students (and themselves!) that their youth group is not the church. It is a ministry—a Sunday school group, really—that is included in the local church. Youth groups get into trouble when they take on a life of their own with separate goals or agendas than the wider church body. A youth ministry that is done well encourages participating in corporate worship, equips students for service

immediately in the wider life of the church and intentionally reminds students that they won't be in a "youth group" for the rest of their lives.

If it is true that the mandate for the discipleship and evangelism of children—from the earliest stages of God's people—comes first to parents, then a youth ministry done well supports, encourages and reinforces the primary ministry role of the Christian family in the lives of students. This means a youth pastor views himself as standing *in support* of godly parents, not *in opposition* to them. There are, of course, circumstances that may demand confronting parents; abuses of parental authority certainly occur. But, in general, pastors for youth stand with parents—partnering with them, and even equipping them, in order to reinforce the biblical and gospel truths that are being taught in the home. A youth pastor who sees himself only as a "youth" pastor has missed the point. Someone who leads a youth ministry well is really a pastor to families. When a youth ministry is done well, it has great value to the life of the local church and to the life-long discipleship and church service of Christian students.[3]

I still believe those words! Youth ministries, in the context of local churches, can be wonderful gifts to students and parents who are seeking to raise their kids to know and love Jesus Christ.

It's been my experience, too, that more and more youth ministries are moving back away from a pure "entertainment" model of youth ministry toward more substantive models that are serious about Scripture and partnership with parents.

How can parents seek to "share" their children when it comes to partnership with youth ministry in the local church?

First, they can *encourage, pray for and support* the youth pastors, directors and workers who serve with their kids. While there may indeed be times to question what is going on in the youth ministry, far too many parents tend to act only as distant critics when it comes to the youth pastor and his ministry in the church.

Only God can keep our children
in Christ and sovereignly see them
through to the end.

Christian parents need to make sure that they're supporting—through prayer and encouragement—the men and women who are teaching their kids the gospel and pointing them toward Christ. Fathers, when was the last time you took your kids' youth pastor out to breakfast to pray for him, encourage him and ask him about his ministry and his family? Mothers, why not seek to pray for and encourage the female youth workers who are mentoring your daughter?

Second, parents can *intentionally partner* with youth ministry in the church, joyfully acting as members of the same "team," rather than as opponents. I realize that this has to be a two-way street; many youth directors need to be pushed and encouraged toward much more engagement and partnership with parents.

But, parents can lead the way here in some cases. Consider contacting the youth minister at your church, for example, and ask him how you might reinforce some of his teaching and preaching in the home. Or see what the youth group needs—in terms of resources or homes for small group meetings—and volunteer your time or help.

Third, there can be an active *inviting* of youth pastors and workers into the lives of our children (assuming they are indeed men and women who love Jesus Christ and are living godly lives).

This means letting youth workers know that you support what they're doing and welcome their involvement in your children's lives. It means letting our children know, too, that you're in favor of them spending time with older people (other than us) who can encourage them in their faith.

Consider having a youth worker over to dinner and getting to know him or her as a whole family. This can be a great step toward "sharing" the discipleship and mentoring of our children, and it may even go a long way in gaining their trust and respect as well!

Mentoring/Discipleship

As someone who had a very healthy relationship with parents who loved and served Jesus Christ, I can say very confidently that, even in such a case, there is a benefit in hearing other voices than only parents with regard to the Christian life and faith in Jesus Christ.

I listened to what my parents said to me, but I sometimes (especially during high school years) listened with a different kind of attentiveness to younger guys who, for example, I saw as models for what I wanted to be in five to ten years. In other words, it was always helpful to have my parents as a shining example to me of faith and life in Christ; it was helpful in a different way to see a twenty-five year-old guy (who I thought was pretty cool) walking vibrantly with Jesus and encouraging me to do the same.

One of my high school basketball coaches, for example, was a godly young man, who modeled very well for me a commitment to Jesus Christ, God's Word and the church. It was extremely helpful for me to see my parents' example but also the example of a younger guy who I considered very "cool," living for Jesus boldly, passionately and genuinely. My parents, as well, were grateful for this godly man's influence in my life as a high school student.

I want to urge Christian parents to consider intentionally opening up their children to mentoring and discipleship relationships with people in the local church *other* than ourselves. Again, if a parent leans toward a "fix my kid!" mentality, this won't be a challenge! But, if a parent tends toward holding their children a bit too tightly and fiercely guarding access to them spiritually, this may be an important, intentional and difficult decision.

The reality is, though, that our kids *are* going to hear voices other than our own—especially as they grow older. They're going to be pulled in other directions . . . away from Jesus and away from His church. The younger years are times to invite other believers into their lives to provide help in mentoring and discipleship.

As parents, we may even find that our kids listen to other people in a different way than they listen to us, even as such people reinforce our convictions about a life devoted to Jesus Christ and involvement in His body, the church.

A Heart Adjustment

I want to give a few final words to those of us for whom this principle is deeply challenging and difficult; those who, ultimately out of deep love and concern for our kids, struggle to "release" their spiritual care to others and invite other people "in" to their mentoring and discipleship. How can we begin to do this "sharing" thing, for the spiritual good of our children and the future of their relationships with Christ?

Be willing to "share" our kids with fellow believers whom God has provided.

It begins, I think, with a prayerful "release" of our children to God's care, which is infinitely more powerful and perfect than our own. This involves a careful and intentionally faith-filled decision to begin asking God to help us hold our children with "open hands" rather than with "clenched fists."

It starts, in other words, in our hearts, as we begin to acknowledge that God alone can do what we sometimes *wish* we could do for our kids: keep them in His love and in the community of believers!

In reality, of course, only God can keep our children in Christ and sovereignly see them through to the end in lives of faithfulness and love for his Son. Listen to the beautiful benediction at the end of Jude—words that speak to God's power to "keep" believers close to Him in faithfulness until the end:

> Now to him who is able to keep you from stumbling
> and to present you blameless before the presence of
> his glory with great joy, to the only God, our Savior,

> through Jesus Christ our Lord, be glory, majesty, dominion, and authority, before all time and now and forever. Amen. (Jude 24–25)

A faith-filled release of our children, involving the "sharing" of them with others, will relate directly to our belief in God's sovereign role in their lives. Far too often, we put ourselves as the subject of those verbs that Jude mentions at the end of his letter.

We think that *we* must keep our kids from stumbling. We wish that *we* could present our kids "blameless" before the glorious God, but we can't. We can teach them. We can train them, but we can't do what only God can do—keep them from stumbling and miraculously present them blameless before God through faith in Jesus Christ. We need to ask God to do this and joyfully invite others into the lives of our kids to help them understand who God is and all He has done.

Conclusion

So, we've come to the end of the fourth of five principles for parenting that relate to raising kids who grow up to love Jesus and "stick" in the church. Here's where we are so far:

- Principle 1: "A Delicate Balance"
  Parents whose children grow up to love Jesus and remain active in the church tend to find the right balance between "helicopter" parent on the one side, and "let it go" parent on the other side. They are actively engaged in their children's lives spiritually, without falling prey to overly obsessive and controlling tendencies.

- Principle 2: "Modeling"

  Parents whose children grow up to love Jesus and remain active in the church tend to "model" well a genuine faith to their children through their own love for and service to the church, humility, and authentic faith and love for spouses and people around them. They "practice what they preach" so that their kids cannot accuse them of hypocrisy.

- Principle 3: "Gospel"

  Parents whose children grow up to love Jesus and remain active in the church tend to be ones who have established a gospel-centered approach to parenting, rather than an approach that is purely moralistic, legalistic, pragmatic or even only theocentric. They seek to infuse daily life with gospel truth, directing their children to, not a religious system, but the person and work of Jesus Christ (death for sins and resurrection from the dead), who alone gives power for obedience, faith, and holiness.

- Principle 4: "Sharing"

  Parents whose children grow up to love Jesus and remain active in the church tend to be ones who have intentionally "shared" their kids with people in the church—of all different ages—who have helped their children know Jesus and learn more about life in Him. They resist the urge to control every aspect of their kids' lives; and instead they actively partner with others who will speak God's truth to their children in winsome and powerful ways, supporting their fundamental work of gospel-centered parenting and discipleship in the home.

By God's grace, may we all commit ourselves to doing everything we can to teach, train and disciple our children toward the love of Jesus Christ and His church. May we also be willing to "share" our kids with fellow believers whom God has provided to befriend, mentor and influence for the sake of God's name.

8

Principle 5: Practicing Friendship

I still remember my father making a very simple statement to my brothers and me when we were younger. It was a statement that was profound and encouraging–far more than I realized at the time.

We were playing some kind of sports game or activity, and he paused for just a moment and said to us: "You know, I *like* you guys."

Sure, my mom and dad told us they loved us all the time, we were well convinced of that fact. What my dad was pausing to remind us was in some ways even more significant than parental love.

He was telling us that he genuinely enjoyed being with us. He liked us. He thought my brothers and I were fun to be around. He would choose to spend time with us even if he didn't have to.

That's a simple statement; it was also quite profound, and important to young boys who loved and admired their dad. I remember, as a young boy, feeling very honored that my dad eally felt that way about us. He liked us. He wasn't just hanging out with us because he had to. That was good for a young boy to hear from his dad.

The final principle of parenting our children toward lasting relationships with Jesus Christ and His church is the principle of *friendship*. It's a principle that is incredibly difficult to get right, because it's so easy to fall off toward one extreme or the other.

But, as I've talked to parents, interviewed pastors and discussed these principles with young adults, I've become more and more convinced that this "friendship" principle belongs here as one of the five pillars.

Without his parents, his true "colors" come out,
and he actually begins to relate to people
and demonstrate his real personality.

It's the parents, generally, who have learned to develop a healthy friendship—a genuine relationship—with their children who have far more often than not been able to steer them toward Jesus Christ, and toward a lasting faith in Him and engagement with His people. So, let's examine this "friendship" principle together.

What Does Friendship in Parenting Look Like?

Here's how I'll describe this "friendship" principle, in very basic terms: Parents whose kids love Jesus and stay in the church tend to develop a genuine, authentic "friendship" relationship with them, which is not devoid of authority or instruction, but is filled with genuine affection, conversation and even fun.

Over and over again, the picture of healthy parent-child relationships, which tend to nurture a growing faith in Jesus Christ, involves a genuine "like" between the parents and the kids. They enjoy being together. They can talk comfortably and honestly with each other. They make jokes. They don't mind hanging out. The best way to describe it is that it's a friendship, as well as a parent-child relationship.

Development

This principle of "friendship" is one that develops and changes in the different stages of childhood and growth (unlike "modeling," for example, which should always be practiced with the same commitment and tenor). Obviously, "friendship" with a four-year-old child is not going to look quite the same as honest and authentic conversations with an eighteen-year-old young adult who is getting ready to go off to college. The need for discipline, oversight and careful instruction will be more pronounced at certain times, of course.

In other words, a dad can talk more "man to man" with his eighteen-year-old son than he can with a toddler. A mother can level with her daughter during her high school years (perhaps based on her experience in high school) in a different way than during a confrontation with a temper-tantrum-throwing three-year-old. The relationship, and the ability to come alongside children, changes and develops with years of growth and maturity.

Even so, I would argue that this "friendship" principle can absolutely be applied from the earliest ages. Your four-year-old daughter needs to know that you "like" her, as well as "love" her. Hopefully, she knows that you will come home every night, take her to the doctor when she is sick, make her dinner and provide her with clothes.

But, from an early age, she needs to know that you enjoy her—that you think she is funny, likable and fun to be around. There's a profound importance in simply playing together, as well as being the "serious" parent (which we all need to be at some times).

Think about the difference between simply dragging a three-year-old little girl around to family events and taking a special trip to the coffee shop for hot chocolate for the specific purpose of talking to *her*. Or, consider the difference between merely saying "I love you" to your five-year-old son as you tuck him into bed at night and taking time once in a while to tell him some of the aspects of his character and personality that you really treasure and enjoy. These are small ways, but they can have a big cumulative effect.

Avoiding Two Extremes

It's probably easy to recognize the different extremes into which parents can fall when it comes to this "friendship" principle. Generally, there will be a tendency toward either overly *authoritative* or overly *peer-like* tendencies. Let's take a moment and consider these.

Authoritative

Parents are given authority from God himself to raise, lead, and train their children in the fear of the Lord. Identifying this "extreme" in parenting is not intended in any way to question this role or responsibility. Children, likewise, are instructed to "honor" their fathers and their mothers, a command that the New Testament repeats and enforces. There is a role of authority and honor that is a given for Christian parents and children.

The fact that the love of one parent would settle on one child and not the other is devastating.

However, there is an extreme leaning, for some parents, toward only interacting with their children on the basis of their authority and never on the basis of genuine relationship or genuine enjoyment.

In other words, the parent-child relationship, in these cases, can become primarily about discipline and instruction, without any true relational connection. The "seriousness" of the role of parent is strongly embraced, so strongly, in fact, that the child never really learns to spend time with the parent in genuine relationship.

In our context, you can sometimes tell when this extreme is at play by the way a given teenager acts around his parents, in contrast with the way he acts apart from them.

With his parents, he might be quiet, submissive and disengaged.

Without his parents, his true "colors" come out, and he actually begins to relate to people and demonstrate his real personality. Sadly, this can indicate a parental relationship that has been overwhelmingly focused on "keeping him in line," without any attempt to engage him relationally. He's been "loved" by parents, but not necessarily "liked" by them.

One student in our high school ministry several years ago, for example, barely said a word to me whenever his parents were around. Once he was in a small group setting, though, he had plenty to say: questions to ask about God's Word, honest confessions about struggles with sin and wonderful insights about living for God in a public high school context.

Create space for genuine conversations with their kids about Jesus, the Bible and the Christian life.

It took me a while to figure out the disconnection between the way he acted around his parents and the way he acted around his peers; finally, it dawned on me that he felt stifled by his parents. He was terrified of saying something of which they would disapprove.

So, he shrunk back into his "shell" whenever they were around. Sadly, this young man's parents had not given him the confidence of knowing that they *liked* him and accepted him for the imperfect, yet growing, young follower of Christ that he was.

Peer-like

The other extreme is equally dangerous, and we've touched on it a bit before in earlier chapters. The "peer-like" approach to parenting is exactly the opposite of what we described above: all relationship with no authority. Here, the authoritative role of parenting (instruction, discipline, training, correction) is largely abandoned, usually in the name of wanting to really have a relationship with the child and to earn his or her trust.

Parents for whom this extreme is the reality often make a point of doing fun things together—shopping, camping trips, excursions to the city—seeking to build a solid friendship with their kids. Often, this can produce a really sweet season of relationship and friendship.

One positive picture of this is an elder in our church who has three daughters whom he has taken out to breakfast *every* Saturday morning for almost their entire lives. There's no "agenda" for these breakfast trips together; it's just time to hang out . . . dad and daughters.

I'm fully convinced that those little breakfast "dates" have had a lot to do with the wonderful health of this man's relationship with his daughters, who are all now walking faithfully with Christ today.

The problem with an extreme move in this direction, of course, begins to emerge when the child needs to be confronted, disciplined or rebuked spiritually.

If there's been no authoritative foundation laid as the ultimate reality in the home, the child is going to be shocked and surprised that her "buddy" is now seriously confronting her—and even disciplining her—because of her sinful behavior and rebellion. She might even feel duped: "I thought we were friends!"

To put it in a slightly different way, if we seek to *only* be friends with our kids, then our spiritual influence in their lives will *only* be at the level of "friend." We'll be in danger of losing the God-given role of authority and spiritual leadership in the lives of our children, which sometimes does need to come with strength, discipline and even punishment.

Biblical Foundations

Many of the biblical examples that we have to support this principle are on the negative side, not the positive side. While we want to avoid saying too much more than Scripture does in these cases, let me highlight just a few of the biblical examples in which a *lack* of this friendship principle (or at least an authentic, caring, genuine relationship between parent and child) led to spiritually devastating results.

Isaac and Jacob

As the story of Isaac and his twin boys is revealed to us in Scripture, it's not too difficult to get a picture of the relationship Jacob had (or didn't have!) with his father. The Scriptures, as usual, don't get too psychological; we don't get the whole inner monologue of Jacob, with his pain and agony and longing for a better relationship with his father. We are simply told that, as he and his twin brother Esau grew older, "Isaac loved Esau . . . but Rebekah loved Jacob" (Gen. 25:28).

What a sad statement! The fact that the love of one parent would settle on one child and not the other is devastating, and it's not difficult to begin to imagine the dysfunction and pain that became the norm in the life of this young family. Surely, Jacob grew up as the "momma's boy," spending time in the tent with Rebekah, but craving a closer friendship and relationship with the more "manly" Isaac.

The results of this failure of Isaac to engage with his son Jacob are obvious—and devastating to his other son, Esau.

With the help of his devious mother, Jacob reacts against Isaac's favoritism and emotional distance by tricking Isaac into blessing him instead of Esau (from whom he has already stolen the family's birthright).

There will come a day for all parents when children will move beyond the scope of their authority.

Of course, God's sovereign hand is in all of this, but in the short-term, this rips apart the family and causes a terrible rift between Jacob and his brother Esau. We begin to wonder if things might have been different if Isaac had pursued a friendship with his son Jacob, just as he obviously invested relationally in his son Esau.

David and Absalom

Again, in the story of David, which is recorded for us in First and Second Samuel, we don't get a ton of details about his parenting "style," or stories about the way he raised his kids.

We do, however, see the disastrous results of at least some of his failures as a father. Most tragic, by far, is the story of his son Absalom, who ended up rebelling against him and losing his life in the pursuit of his father's crown. It doesn't end well for young, handsome Absalom!

It seems, though, that the trajectory of Absalom's life begins to be set many years before he actually rises up to try to take the kingdom from his father. After the terrible and tragic rape of his sister Tamar by another one of David's sons, Amnon, Absalom stews in anger for quite some time.

Then, seeing that David isn't going to do anything about Amnon's terrible crime, Absalom takes matters into his own hands; he tricks Amnon into a meeting away from the palace and has him stabbed to death.

Again, David is distant; he sends Absalom away but neither confronts him directly nor punishes him sternly. Finally, Absalom gets to come back into the presence of King David, but a significant relationship surely is never forged.

They've built a foundation for a Christ-centered friendship.

At best, David seems to be a distant father; at worst, he's probably negligent in his duty to earnestly engage his children with God's Word and God's truth in the context of deep relationship. If the great King David—he who was called a man after God's own heart—can fail in this way, then certainly we can all be susceptible toward failure in relationship and friendship with our children.

Benefits of Friendship

There are definitely some benefits to pursuing a deep friendship with our children, while, of course, maintaining the balance between proper authority and peer-level interaction. As I've had conversations with parents, pastors and young adults who have grown up and stayed in the church, here are some of the benefits of a right balance in friendship that have emerged.

Authentic Gospel Conversations

A foundation of deep relationship and friendship in a parent-child relationship can lead to authentic gospel conversations. I'm not talking about these conversations as being in a completely different category from family devotions and more intentional times of teaching and instruction in God's Word. All Christian parents are called to these at some level. There is something that all parents whose kids grow up to love both Jesus and the church have in common: They have genuine conversations with their kids about matters relating to faith in Jesus and life in obedience to Him, and they intentionally create "space" for honest questions, earnest engagement and even doubts and struggles.

Let me put this in slightly different terms. Parents who tend to lean toward extreme authority and discipline—without a pursuit of friendship and relationship—often also relegate gospel-centered conversations and biblical topics to the realm of teaching (teaching "at" their children). For parents who lean in that general direction, I'm advocating for an intentional decision to create space for genuine conversations with their kids about Jesus, the Bible and the Christian life.

In my experience, and in light of the conversations I've had with parents and Christian kids, these conversations about Jesus, standing in the kitchen late at night, can sometimes have the most significant shaping effects on life, faith and relationship with Jesus.

One family in our church, for example, has struggled with rebellion from several of their children. The more I got to know and understand their situation, the more I realized that the biblical "teaching" and "training" they gave to their children over the years was a lot more like stern lectures than friendly, warm along-the-way kind of conversations.

Lectures about the Bible and faith—however truthful they may be—will not have their desired effect if they are not rooted in a relationship of warmth, love and trust.

Genuine Relationship

Next, a pursuit of friendship with our kids—learning to "like" them as well as "love" them—forges a genuine relationship with them. "Genuine relationship" is a direct antonym to a "forced" or "formal" relationship that only exists because of family organization and structure.

Far too many kids who grow up to reject both Jesus and the church do so out of frustration with their parents. They have, sadly, linked and identified God with their distant and stand-offish parents, the people with whom they crave a deeper and more genuine relationship.

Perhaps the first and best way we can teach our kids about the intimate and personal love of God for them is to engage them in every way we can in deep and authentic relationship.

Get to know them.

Listen to them.

Ask them questions.

Even as we lead them with authority and discipline, they should never be able to say that we were uninterested in having a deep and close relationship with them!

A Way Back After Rebellion

The foundation of friendship and relationship for which I'm advocating can also lead to a way "back" to faith in God and love for the church, after a season of rebellion and sin. The reality is that we are raising children with sinful natures and naturally rebellious hearts; there will be some who—despite our best efforts to point them to Christ—choose to go their own way for a season (sometimes a long season).

The wonderful reality of a loving and genuine friendship centered on the gospel of Jesus Christ is that it provides a path back "in" when God brings an older child to repentance after such a season.

Be a co-laborer for Jesus, as well as a teacher of the things of God.

There's a natural path back into relationship with parents and with Christ and his church. We might be reminded, on this point, of Jesus' parable of the prodigal son (see Luke 15). Surely, it was this son's confidence in the gracious character of his father that enabled him to find hope in a return to his home . . . even after years of sin and rebellion.

I talked to one young adult who is currently finishing college for whom this applied perfectly! There was a period of intense cynicism, bitterness toward the church and rebellious behavior in this person's life during high school although not an outright rejection of the gospel.

Throughout the whole process, his parents continued to engage with him in deep relationship and genuine conversation, even as they rebuked him and called him to repentance. Today, as he's back in step with both Jesus and the local church, he looks back on his parents' friendship with him as a key part of his journey to repentance.

One thing he was never able to do—even in his most bitter and cynical moments—was question their deep love—and "like"—for him, as they pursued him in loving relationship and friendship.

Very simply, they never stopped being his parents. They were always available to talk, always gracious and generous and never unfair, even when they exerted "tough love," rebuke and discipline.

A Path into Adulthood

The final benefit of pursuing a friendship with our kids is that it gives us a kind of "path" into the right kind of relationship with them as they enter adulthood. There will come a day for all parents when children will move beyond the scope of their authority, even as they are called to continue to honor and love their parents.

For children who have known the authority of strict parents, without genuine relationship or friendship, this transition is not always a pleasant one—for parents or children.

Many times, when the "formality" of the parent-child relationship is removed, it's revealed that there is no deep relationship to maintain a bond and friendship during adult years. How sad this is when it happens!

Yet, for parents who have sought to nurture a friendship with their children—even during their growing-up years—there can be a beautiful shift that occurs during young adulthood. It's a shift from parent as "leader" to parent as "trusted advisor." Conversations can become even richer, as the child begins to make big decisions about life, career, schooling and dating and marriage.

Many parents can look forward to a sweet stage of relationship with their children at this point, as "befriended" children turn back to them for counsel, advice, wisdom, prayer and encouragement.

While they never cease to be parents, they've laid a natural "path" for the emergence of their relationship with their children into the adult years. They've built a foundation for a Christ-centered friendship, which can continue to mark their children for Christ long after they've left the direct authority of parents in the home behind.

A Way Forward

Let me offer just a few practical ways forward for parents, as they seek to pursue—with balance—deep relationship and friendship with their children for the glory of Jesus and their spiritual good. Here are just a few practical tips:

Get to Know Them

Consider making a new commitment, right now, to really getting to know your kids well. When you're with them . . . engage with them fully. Look them in the eye and interact with them (without checking your e-mail on your phone at the same time!). Figure out what makes them "tick." Find out why they like what they like. Let them know you're interested in them.

Ask Questions

There are times to teach (and we all much teach Scripture and the truths of the gospel to our kids), but there are also times to ask them questions as well.

Draw out their thoughts, feelings and perceptions about people and the world. "What are you struggling with today?" "What are you most excited about in your life right now?" "What's the hardest part for you about following Jesus?"

Again, be interested in them with genuine excitement and earnestness.

These principles will be helpful to you as you seek to raise your children to know and love the Lord Jesus Christ.

Let Them Know You Like Them

Find ways to let them know that you actually like being with them (not just that you love them because you're supposed to). Laugh at their jokes. Choose to spend time together. Tell them you enjoy their company.

Show Affection

I know that some of us struggle with this! But even if our kids try to squirm out of hugs, or turn bright red when we say "I love you" in public, it's worth it. They appreciate it. They need it, even when they don't show it.

Admit You're Growing

With regard to the gospel of Jesus Christ and life in Him, let them know that you're "in it" with them. Remind them that you are still learning—and tell them what you're learning about God. Remind them that you're fighting sin and pursuing holiness—and tell them what that looks like. Be a co-laborer for Jesus, as well as a teacher of the things of God.

Conclusion

Well, we have reached the end of Part I of this book and the five principles for effective Christian parenting. Here's what we have learned:

- Principle 1: "A Delicate Balance"
  Parents whose children grow up to love Jesus and remain active in the church tend to find the right balance between "helicopter" parent on the one side and "let it go" parent on the other side. They are actively engaged in their children's lives spiritually, without falling prey to overly obsessive and controlling tendencies.

- Principle 2: "Modeling"
  Parents whose children grow up to love Jesus and remain active in the church tend to "model" well a genuine faith to their children through their own love for and service to the church, humility and authentic faith and love for spouses and people around them. They "practice what they preach" so that their kids cannot accuse them of hypocrisy.

- Principle 3: "Gospel"
  Parents whose children grow up to love Jesus and remain active in the church tend to be ones who have established a gospel-centered approach to parenting, rather than an approach that is purely moralistic, legalistic, pragmatic or even only theocentric. They seek to infuse daily life with gospel truth, directing their children to, not a religious system, but the person and work of Jesus Christ (death for sins and resurrection from the dead), who alone gives power for obedience, faith and holiness.

- Principle 4: "Sharing"
  Parents whose children grow up to love Jesus and remain active in the church tend to be ones who have intentionally "shared" their kids with people in the church—of all different ages—who have helped their children know Jesus and learn more about life in Him. They resist the urge to control every aspect of their kids' lives, and instead they actively partner with others who will speak God's truth to their children in winsome and powerful ways, supporting their fundamental work of gospel-centered parenting and discipleship in the home.

- Principle 5: "Friendship"
  Parents whose children grow up to love Jesus and remain active in the church tend to be ones who have pursued deep friendships with their children. They have pursued them in deep and authentic relationship, without ever sacrificing their roles of authority, teaching, training and instruction in the faith. Their children grow up knowing that their parents "like" them as well as "love" them, and

the genuine relationship that results can, at least, not be used against the faith or the church.

By God's grace, I pray that these principles will be helpful to you as you seek to raise your children to know and love the Lord Jesus Christ and to serve His body, the church, in the coming years.

Now, let's get to some instructions and biblical thoughts for parents at all stages of their children's development (in light of these five principles). Then, let's turn to some guidance for both parents and the church regarding children who have walked away from the faith.

PART TWO

9

A Way Forward

At this point, we have established the principles for gospel-centered parenting. As noted, these principles have emerged from observations, interviews and my general pastoral experience with young people who have grown up in Christian homes and the church and have continued in faith in Jesus Christ and involvement in the local church during their college and young adult years. Hopefully, you've found these principles to be helpful. I certainly view them as foundational to the way I'm seeking to raise my own children as a Christian father.

Now, let's apply these principles in a few different ways. First, in this chapter, I want to "flesh out" the principles in some very tangible ways, as we examine a few different stages of the development, growth and maturity of young people. Then, in the final three chapters, I'll turn to some words of counsel for the church, for parents who feel like they're on the "other side" of the focus of this book (parents whose children have seemingly abandoned the faith) and, finally, for young people (pre-college) themselves. It's my hope that these final chapters will serve to expand and further apply some of the key points I've made in examination of this important topic.

Stages

The simple reality is that the five principles we've explored—Delicate Balance, Modeling, Gospel, Sharing, Friendship—are going to be applied in different ways at each stage of our children's growth and development. Friendship with our sixteen-year-old is going to look quite different than friendship with our two-year-old!

You are setting a course with the rhythm of your family life.

Probably, a four-year-old is going to receive a lot more "hands-on" instruction and protection than would be appropriate for a fourteen-year-old.

Let's consider just some of the ways these biblical principles for parenting could work themselves out at various stages.

Pre-Kids

I want to start, actually, by addressing the "pre-kid" stage of marriage, young married couples who have not yet had children and are beginning to consider having children. Hopefully there are some of you who are reading this book, as part of the way that you are thoughtfully preparing ahead of time to be godly and intentional Christian parents. While some of the principles discussed here will not be applicable until you have children, there are two of them that you can begin practicing right now in order to lay a foundation for raising children to God's glory.

The first is the principle of "Modeling." You can commit to living, serving, talking and engaging with your church *now*, in precisely the way that you want your children to observe in the years to come.

Far too often, it is the birth of a child that begins to "wake up" Christian parents up to the need to re-engage in church involvement, family devotions and regular prayer in the home. It can lead to an awkward, and often difficult, time of trying to unlearn bad spiritual habits—and to develop good ones—for the sake of the kids. Sadly, we see this all too often in our church context.

In such cases, often the transition from a somewhat self-centered childless marriage to a Christ-centered child-filled marriage is never quite accomplished; the gospel-centered foundation of the home was simply not established soon enough during the "pre-kid" years. As we all know, habits are difficult to make . . . and even more difficult to break!

Let me encourage pre-kid Christian couples to begin establishing some gospel-centered and church-focused habits in the home right now—before the children come. Attend church together, join a small group and begin serving in the children's or youth ministry.

Establish a time for family prayer or devotions, even though the "family" is just made up of the two of you at this point. Set some parameters for television watching; consider reading something together and praying before bed. Intentionally discuss Sunday's sermon over a seated Sunday lunch. All of these are simply examples of ways that you can begin preparing, and even "practicing," to be a family whose roots are in the local church and whose focus is the gospel of Jesus Christ.

You are setting a course with the rhythm of your family life that will lead you toward the right kind of "modeling" for your children who have not yet entered your home and your life.

Babies

Ah, the baby stage! As I write this, our youngest is still in diapers, drinking from a bottle and still very much dependent on Mom and Dad for literally everything. We love this little child with all our hearts, and we are committed to protecting her, caring for her, comforting her and loving her. There's nothing like the baby stage, although it certainly comes with its challenges (lack of sleep is one big one!). But sometimes we find it hard to know how to pray for our baby . . . right now.

We pray that she will come to know Jesus in the years to come, and I even take time to pray regularly that God would be—somewhere in the world—raising up a godly and gospel-centered husband for her in the years to come. But, how do we pray for our baby, at a spiritual level, right now?

More than this, how do we interact with a baby on a *spiritual level* during these months and years? How do the principles of this book apply to mothers and fathers whose child or children are in diapers and are unable to speak their first words or take their first steps?

First, let me suggest that protection and security and love are not unspiritual lessons for even a baby to learn. What I mean is this: It is spiritually good for the first awareness of a baby to be the security, warmth and love of kind and protective parents. This, beautifully, is part of God's intention for bringing up children.

While a ten-month-old child, for example, cannot yet fully articulate the gospel of Jesus Christ, he or she can certainly begin to have the consciousness of being loved, protected, nourished and encouraged.

Even these early "senses" of love and security can begin the foundation of a child's sense of a good, loving and protective Heavenly Father.

Pray BIG spiritual prayers for your infants, in hopes that they will sense the BIG love of God for them.

Let's remember that just as bad parents can skew a child's perception of who God is, good parents can help a child understand the nature of a far greater Heavenly "parent."

Second, don't underestimate what speaking and singing can do in the life and heart of an infant!

Talking quietly to a child about Jesus' love for him or her, singing hymns and choruses about God's Word and truth and even reading children's Bible story books to a young baby can be part of beginning to introduce our kids to the things of God. Young parents can, and should, make a commitment to acquaint their children with the stories and songs of the Christian faith even long before they can understand every aspect of them.

Third (more on this at the end of this chapter), parents of infants can pray big-minded spiritual prayers for their little ones. I want to challenge young parents to fill your prayers with spiritual substance, not merely pleas for physical protection! Ask God to begin to reveal Himself to your children—even at very young ages.

Pray that He would begin drawing them to Himself, by the power of His Holy Spirit, from the earliest seasons of life. Pray BIG spiritual prayers for your infants, in hopes that they will sense the BIG love of God for them in Christ in their very early years.

Toddlers

Our church's former director of disability ministries, Dawn Clark, once explained to me her hopes and prayers for the faith and conversion of people in her ministry with severe mental and learning disabilities.

She was realistic; she knew that not every man and woman in their program would be able to articulate the gospel in the way that another member of our congregation could.

Her prayer, as she explained it to me, was that these dear men and women would "say yes to everything about Jesus that they could understand." That is, I think, a wonderful explanation of the response of true faith at every stage of life. What we are hoping and praying for—in the lives and hearts of our toddlers—is that they begin to respond to what they *can* understand about God and the gospel with a hearty "yes!"

At this phase, one way this can begin to work itself out is in their response to authority. As toddlers learn that they are *not* the ones in charge, they begin to be faced with a very important choice: submit to the leadership and "rule" of their parents, or face the disappointment and discipline of Mom and Dad.

This is an important lesson for toddlers to learn, and I would argue that it is a distinctly *spiritual* lesson. It's a very initial step in the direction of their submission to a Creator . . . who is much bigger than they are and who is, in reality, very much "in charge."

More specific to our principles, though, the "toddler" phase of parenting becomes a time to begin establishing many different practices that relate to these.

It's a time of beginning to establish a "friendship" with our kids—playing with them, laughing with them, being interested in them and genuinely engaging with them (as opposed to merely "taking care" of them).

It's a time of beginning to "model" what it looks like to live as a follower of Jesus Christ, setting an example for patterns of speech, loving and respectful actions toward other members of the family and kind and gentle interactions with all people.

It's a time of beginning to "share" influence in our toddlers' lives with brothers and sisters from the local church body who can begin to demonstrate love, care and biblical teaching in their lives. What a wonderful season to begin introducing our children to the community of faith in the church!

Of course, it's the "gospel" principle that can beautifully begin to take shape during the toddler years. Even in the instructions and discipline of parenting, a young toddler can begin to grasp the concept of grace and forgiveness, which can begin to lay a foundation for an understanding of the gracious work of Jesus Christ. Saying "I forgive you" can never come too early in parenting, even if "forgiveness" is not a concept that the toddler totally grasps. These are the days when the earliest formations of the message of Jesus begin to take shape in their minds; take advantage of every conversation for the sake of their knowledge of the Savior.

Pre-School

The years between three and five are incredible ones. My wife and I are in the midst of these years with two of our children even as I write this now.

To say that kids are like "sponges" during these years is a massive understatement; they "soak up" everything and are amazingly responsive to conversation, teaching, learning and early forms of reasoning and logic. They are watching you, parents, with intensity and earnest interest during these years.

Because of this, the "modeling" principle comes into play in a very big way here. These are the years during which Christian parents must ensure that they are living out gospel faith—both outside and inside the home.

These are the days to begin talking to our kids about not only *what* we do regarding Christian faith, church involvement and gospel witness . . . but also *why* we do it (a deep love for Jesus, a desire for others to know him, a passion for building up other believers in their faith, etc.).

Don't get frustrated by all the questions that children in this phase ask; view their rapid-fire inquisitions as opportunities to engage them with the gospel of Jesus Christ. They are interested in hearing from you; take advantage of this!

The "friendship" principle, too, is of massive import during these years. From my personal experience, I can tell you that my four-year-old daughter absolutely needs to know that I like her, think she's funny and enjoy playing games with her . . . and simply being with her. We're developing a friendship—one that I'm convinced will have huge returns in the years to come.

Children need to know that their parents are ultimately "for" them.

Of course, I need to discipline her, tell her no and rebuke her when she is rebellious or disobedient. But, I remain convinced that this God-given role of authority is absolutely compatible with a growing friendship with my daughter, who should be securely delighting in a father who delights in her just the way God has made her.

Finally, the "sharing" principle in this season expands in a large way as well. Kids begin to become more aware of friendships and relationships with kids and adults outside of their immediate families, and such people begin to have influence in their lives. Now is the time to embrace this, rather than resist it.

Find godly families with whom you can connect and whose kids you can connect to your kids. Encourage Sunday school teachers, and thank them for the spiritual role of teaching they are playing in your pre-school kids' lives.

Finally, encourage your own child to listen to the words of other believers in the church, and teach them to be thankful to God for the body of Christ. By God's grace, this can be a season during which your child begins to experience the fellowship of believers in the context of your local church and thrive because of it.

Grade School/Junior High

It is, of course, very difficult to make too many generalizations about this "phase" of growth for kids from Christian families because so much happens between first grade and eighth grade! However, let me just point out a few ways that the five principles can begin to be applied in new ways during these years.

Delicate balance. It's through these developing grade school years that Christian parents often struggle the most with when to "let go" and when to seek to control and dictate the actions and decisions of their children. Of course, during the early grade school years, careful oversight, instruction and monitoring of behavior will be necessary.

Yet, as these years go on, it will be important to actively seek opportunities to encourage growing children to think on their own, making decisions that are not simply dictated to them by their parents. Especially as the junior high years approach, parents should be looking for more and more "fruit" from their kids in terms of real choices and decisions that they are making on the basis of a relationship with Jesus.

There's no "formula" for this, but the general mindset needs to be toward not "doing faith" for our kids, but encouraging them to nurture their own relationship with Jesus as they seek Him personally.

Modeling. There can be some frustrating times during the junior high years; we've certainly witnessed this in the homes of many from our church context! And these certainly won't be years during which children delight to do and imitate every word and action of their parents. (Often, it will probably be quite the opposite.) Yet these are years during which a steady commitment to "practicing what we preach" as Christian parents will be absolutely essential.

While rebellious—and even angry—moments may come, a consistency of character and integrity during these years must stand as a steady witness to our kids that we really believe, with all of our hearts, what we are calling them to believe. A passionate devotion to Jesus Christ must be evident during these sometimes difficult years.

Friendship. The development of relationship throughout the grade school and junior high years can be a significant accompaniment to gospel-driven discipleship; a lack of relationship can greatly damage the effect of our words and teaching. These are years during which family devotions should always be "balanced" by camping trips, movie "dates" or special activities together.

Necessary "lectures" should always be measured with times of joking and laughter. It's hard for even the most stubborn junior higher to reject and deny a mother or father who is genuinely interested in the things he or she loves, values and enjoys.

Gospel. It's also during the grade school and junior high years that kids can begin sniffing out legalism and moralism, as opposed to true biblical and gospel-centered foundations in the family and home.

Rules for the sake of rules will begin to be rebuffed, questioned and rejected; cynicism and anger can even begin to set in during the later grade school years. All of this makes the gospel foundation for the rules and commitments of a Christian family all the more important.

Parents in this season will need to be intentional about constantly explaining the "why" for their commitments, convictions and instructions. Discipline (and there will need to be discipline!) should come with conviction and care, not merely anger and a sense of "retribution."

It has everything to do with their ability
and intentionality to live out the Gospel in
front of their children.

Children need to know that their parents are ultimately "for" them—and for a vibrant relationship with Jesus Christ. It's not simply about keeping the rules, but about knowing Jesus and living for Him . . . which is of eternal significance.

Sharing. What a joy it will be, especially during the later grade school years, for parents to begin to identify godly Christian people (teenagers, young adults and older adults) who can help them to disciple, mentor and teach their children about Scripture and the gospel of Jesus Christ! These are years to begin welcoming this additional influence even more—and perhaps even giving our kids some "say" in it.

For example, if there is a godly college student (of the same gender) in your local church congregation, you may see if he or she would be willing to meet regularly with your junior high student for Bible study, prayer and relational connections. It will help if it's someone whom your child thinks is "cool."

This is one great example of actively and intentionally beginning to "share" the spiritual formation of your children with members of the body of Christ. We need help in this after all!

High School

The high school years, for many, become the "trajectory setting" years with regard to a commitment to Jesus Christ and the local church. While many children from Christian families have professed faith at earlier ages, high school becomes a time when they are forced to decide whether or not they really want to follow Jesus completely . . . with friends often pulling them in very different directions.

This means that high school can be a scary time for many Christian parents; it also makes it a time of great spiritual opportunity! Let me explain.

With regard to our five principles from earlier in the book, the high school years become a fertile field for applying those in fully developed ways. Modeling of the Christian faith, by parents, takes full shape; parents are able to talk openly and honestly about their own relationship with Christ and growth in sanctification.

The delicate balance between "helicopter" parent and "let it go" parent can be applied carefully and thoughtfully, as high school students often have much more freedom with regard to their schedules and social patterns.

Sharing ascends to a new level of importance, as parents have the opportunity to support and encourage the church's work in youth ministry and discipleship. Friendship can grow, as more and more frank and honest conversations can happen about life, relationships and the application of the gospel to every area of life. Of course, the gospel principle, at the center of it all, can continue to guide parents in this stage with regard to their "big picture" leadership and guidance of their children.

If I might speak anecdotally for a moment, let me suggest that what my own parents did *best* during my high school "season" of life was to invite open, honest and frank discussions about all parts of life, in light of the gospel of Jesus Christ.

They didn't make me feel stupid; they openly engaged me with regard to the questions I had about other worldviews, relational issues and topics that related to Scripture and the Christian faith.

They did this in a way that was neither forced, nor contrived; our conversations about theological and biblical issues flowed out of real life.

A conversation about a topic in a high school psychology class would "morph" into a consideration of sin and depravity. An advice talk about a dating relationship would immediately be connected to the pursuit of holiness and sexual purity, for the sake of loving Jesus.

Our relationship was not a "closed system," although my parents certainly maintained full leadership and authority in the home. But I *always* felt that I could approach them and share honestly my thoughts, doubts, struggles and even sinful behavior.

I had confidence that I would be received according to God's Word and God's gospel . . . and not merely according to a legalistic "system" of their own making.

College

If the "trajectory setting" years begin in high school, the trajectory of a young man or woman's life begins to be "set" in college. For the first time, college-age students are beginning to function (mostly) as independent men and women. They set their own schedules, choose their activities and commitments and experience a new "freedom" from their parents.

Spiritually speaking, they are completely free to choose how, when or if they will engage in personal Bible reading and prayer, and where, when or if they will attend church.

I'm seeking to actively trust God for His work in their lives and hearts in drawing them to Him.

It's during the college years that what is inside their hearts (with regard to a relationship with Christ) will begin to make its way to the outside (their actions, choices and commitments).

As such, these can be tough years for many Christian parents, as some experience the pain that comes through seeing one's child begin to stray from Jesus Christ and obedience to Him.

Let me save my comments for that particular situation and make just a few general comments here related to the principles.

First, we've observed in our church's college ministry the great fruit that comes from Christian parents who have mastered that delicate balance between "helicopter" and "let it go" parenting in the lives of their children.

The healthiest and most committed college-age students that we see are those who have been guided and instructed by godly parents, without being dominated and stifled by them.

This has nothing to do with the parents' personal level of commitment to Jesus Christ and the gospel; please understand this!

But, it has everything to do with their ability and intentionality to live out the gospel in front of their children, while inviting them to embrace Jesus on their own—in real, personal and intentional commitment.

Next, let me add that the college years are ones in which the friendship between parents and children can be nurtured, developed and grown like never before—and in a way that will lay a foundation for future years of deep and meaningful relationship.

By the college years, most of the work of discipline and training has been done, although instruction and guidance will most certainly continue.

Because of this, the college years should feel like a time of transition for the relationship between parent and child—moving from purely parent/child into more of a level of mentoring that is fueled by mutual respect.

Let me urge all parents to use these years to build a new "level" onto the relationships with their children. Talk to them as young adults; nurture a deep, gospel-centered friendship with them. This will serve you very well in the years to come.

Young Adult

We'll spend an entire chapter addressing parents whose children have "walked away" from the faith or the church during their young adult years. Here, let me just suggest that parents of young adults tend to move toward one of two extremes with regard to their relationships with their children—especially in the midst of some kind of conflict in the relationship.

The first extreme I'll call the "Love above all else!" extreme. Parents who move in this direction place the peace and health of the relationship with their children above all else . . . no matter what behavior or beliefs are being embraced and practiced by those children. They tend to get a bit "wishy-washy" in terms of their biblical and theological commitments, beginning to talk more about experience than about God's truth and God's Word.

For the sake of maintaining a relationship with their child, they forego any confrontation, rebuke or counsel based on God's Word. They'd rather stay silent and ignore sin, rebellion or a rejection of the church.

The other extreme I'll call "Truth above all else!" Parents who lean this way have no problem calling out the sin and mistakes that their young adult children are making in relationships, behavior and lifestyles; in fact, they do it all the time, and with very little subtlety! Sadly, too many parents do this without any regard for the maintenance of a lasting and healthy relationship with their children.

It's truth with no love—a conviction that is fueled more by anger than by hearts that yearn for their children to know, love and worship the Lord Jesus Christ. The reality is that young adult children can sniff out intentions; they generally don't respond well to an impassioned lecture that sounds angry and vindictive.

There is a middle way, I think. Parents who follow Jesus and live under the authority of God's Word need to continue to call out sin and address mistakes in the lives of their young adult children; I'm convinced of this. To remain silent as our children turn away from Christ and His church is to abdicate one of our most important roles as parents—even into our children's adult years.

What greater joy could we have, as followers of Jesus Christ, than to see our children walking in worship and obedience to the only true Savior and Lord!

But, to confront and rebuke as a "knee-jerk" reaction, without tact, love and gentleness, can permanently damage our relationship with our children, and even alienate them for years. Young adult children need to be firmly convinced, I think, of two unshakeable realities when it comes to their parents:

First, the relationship is intact . . . no matter what. Nothing will change their parents' desire to be with them, talk with them and demonstrate love and maintain a relationship with them.

Second, the commitment to Jesus Christ is primary . . . no relational strain or awkwardness (or sin!) is going to prevent their parents from sharing their biblical and Christ-centered convictions about the most eternally important realities of life. When we hold these two convictions in perfect (or close-to-perfect) tension, we are laying a foundation for a continuing relationship with our adult children, even when they do turn down sinful or unwise paths.

The Role of Prayer

You might have noticed that, as we moved though this discussion of each "phase" of parenting, I said very little about the role of prayer. That's not because it's not important; it's actually because a commitment to prayer should dominate and permeate our parenting in each and every phase! The best application of these parenting principles, without the life-giving work of God the Holy Spirit in our children's lives and hearts, will be completely ineffective and worthless.

At our very best, all we can do is put our children in the place to hear God's Word and be transformed as *God* regenerates their hearts and leads them to repentance, faith in His Son and lives of holiness by His strength and power.

In light of this, let me offer a few exhortations with regard to prayer for our children at every phase of their growth and development.

Pray Regularly

The apostle Paul begins his first letter to the Thessalonians with these words: "We give thanks to God always for all of you, constantly mentioning you in our prayers, remembering before our God and Father your work of faith and labor of love and steadfastness of hope in our Lord Jesus Christ" (1 Thess. 1:2–3). According to the pattern of the great apostle, our prayers for our children ought to be constant—daily.

Yes, there are principles for parenting, which I have put forward in this book, and I pray that these are helpful and beneficial to you! But spiritually speaking, there is no better work that you can do on your children's behalf than to offer up prayers to God for their lives every single day.

In my own life, I've recently made a commitment to pray for each of my children every morning. I'm seeking to actively trust God for his work in their lives and hearts in drawing them to Him. I've also found that this regular commitment to prayer for them—even at the start of each day—changes the way that I approach each new day as I relate to them.

Place our trust in Him—the only One who holds their lives and hearts with power, grace, love and sovereignty.

It makes me a bit more conscious of my words to them and interactions with them; it reminds me to be intentional about the way I "back up" my prayers with gospel-centered instruction and grace-filled leadership of them.

Let's pray for our children every single day, trusting that God alone holds the power to transform their hearts and lives and make them obedient to Christ Jesus.

Pray Spiritually

Many parents, I fear, pray for their children regularly, but fail to pray deeply spiritual prayers for them. Some, for example, focus primarily on physical protection ("Lord, please protect Julia this day as she travels . . . etc."). Others might focus mainly on growth, health, and success—asking God to help their children in school, sports, work or music. Then, there can even be a slight distinction between praying "moral" prayers and prayers that are truly "gospel-shaped" in their spiritual focus.

What I mean here is the distinction between prayers for our kids to "behave" ("Lord, please help Tommy to make the right choices today . . . ") and prayers that are focused on the Spirit-empowered transformation of their hearts ("Lord, would you, by your Spirit, help Sarah grow in her knowledge and love for the Lord Jesus Christ today . . . ").

On this point, again, we might look to the example of Paul as he prayed for the early churches (his spiritual "children" in Christ).

> For this reason, because I have heard of your faith in the Lord Jesus and your love toward all the saints, I do not cease to give thanks for you, remembering you in my prayers, that the God of our Lord Jesus Christ, the Father of glory, may give you a spirit of wisdom and of revelation in the knowledge of him, having the eyes of your hearts enlightened, that you may know what is the hope to which he has called you, what are the riches of his glorious inheritance in the saints, and what is the immeasurable greatness of his power toward us who believe. (Eph. 1:15–19)

This is a huge, spiritually-focused prayer from Paul, to be sure. And so, the question would be: Are you praying prayers for your children that are not only regular, but deeply spiritual? Are you asking God to do, by His Spirit, what you can never accomplish simply through your leadership, instruction and guidance, that is, change and transform the hearts and souls of your kids toward the worship of Jesus Christ? Parents, let's commit to praying BIG spiritual prayers for our children. D.A. Carson's book, *Praying with Paul*,[1] would be a wonderful resource for this commitment.

Pray Earnestly

Finally, pray *earnestly* for your children. I mean with passion, intensity, and tears and pleading . . . if necessary. What greater joy could we have, as followers of Jesus Christ, than to see our children walking in worship and obedience to the only true Savior and Lord!

Our prayers for our kids ought to be passionate pleas to God, as we actively and humbly place our trust in Him—the only one who holds their lives and hearts with power, grace, love and sovereignty.

I would urge you to prioritize this kind of prayer, if you are not doing so already. Make space for pleading, earnest prayers for your children in your life. You may find that this strengthens your own faith and love for God as well!

Conclusion

While there is certainly no easy formula for beginning to apply all that we have talked about thus far, I do hope I've been able "flesh out" a bit what some of the biblical principles of this book can, and should, look like at the various stages of your children's lives.

By God's grace, it is my earnest prayer that you will seek to apply these principles thoughtfully and graciously during each season of parenting.

And, my hope is that—with every step—you will be pouring out prayers to our gracious God that He will work powerfully in your children's lives to draw them to Him . . . for His glory and their eternal good in Christ.

10

For the Church

This book began with a focus on college-age and young adult men and women. It's really with regard to this age group that many of the recent studies have caused widespread panic across those in the evangelical church.

Are we losing our young people? Why are we not reaching our twentysomethings? What can we do to counteract this mass exodus of millennials who are walking out the doors of our churches, never to return? Hopefully, this book has helped to counteract some of the panic that certain statistics can cause.

My prayer, too, is that this discussion has been encouraging, as I've sought to demonstrate the ways that godly parents all over our country (and our world, by God's grace) are raising children who do indeed grow up to love and cherish Jesus Christ and serve His church. Still, the general problem of "losing" twentysomethings in the context of local churches remains. In relatively large, multi-generational evangelical congregations, especially ones with older and well-established leadership structures, we are beginning to see the "career-aged" folks slipping through the cracks of ministry, training, involvement and service in the context of the church. I don't think this should be the case. It certainly doesn't have to be.

A Shift in Audience

Up until now, I've been writing mainly for Christian parents of children of all ages (and even to young couples who have not yet begun to have children).

I've sought to lay out some of the central findings—in the form of "principles"—about children who tend to grow up in Christian families in the church into adulthood, and stay engaged with faith in Jesus and involvement and service in a local congregation.

Young people in their twenties make up the future of our churches.

My hope has been to help Christian parents see, from the perspective of someone who has served for several years in student ministries, the common traits of such young adults.

Now my intended audience is shifting. I'm speaking to local churches: pastors, elders, deacons and lay leaders. How do we reach, disciple, engage, train and send out our college and career-age folks that are in our churches?

Why Must We Reach and Equip Young Adults?

Before we answer that "how?" question (and it's a very big one), we need to address the "why?" question. Why is it so important for us to engage our young adults now, rather than waiting for them to start serving and leading in our churches during their middle-aged years?

I once wrote about the intense need for engaging our young adults right now, about the involvement, training and excitement of a very specific contingent of our church population: the young, single, twentysomethings of our church bodies. (From this point onward, I will refer to them as the "career folks.")

In my estimation, and in the estimation of many elders, pastors and key lay leaders of local churches around the country, this is our biggest current "miss" in established, multi-generational church ministries.

Even as family ministry, adult ministries and youth ministries continue to generally thrive in local church congregations, the situation of the career folks is troubling for at least three reasons.

1. People in the early stages of their career in our congregations have the potential to either become the next generation of key leaders, teachers, elders and deacons or to create a serious generational leadership void in the coming years if they all go other places to worship. We run the risk of missing an opportunity to *train up the next generation* of godly men and women who will carry on the work of the gospel of Jesus Christ in and through our local church congregations.

2. These same early-career people in our congregations are—in many ways—the best and most immediately equipped to build the church congregation

evangelistically. Many of them spend the majority of their weeks in secular workplaces and have close relationships with many other career people who do not know Jesus and who are open to spiritual conversations during their single and more mobile/flexible years.

3. They have incredible potential to guide us as a church in innovation, creativity and contextualization of gospel ministry even right now. Even before many of these men and women may be ready to step into significant leadership roles, we need to be *learning from their insights* now, with regard to how we as a church can better engage and reach our culture with the gospel of Jesus Christ.

You can begin to see some of the huge potential I see for reaching our career-aged folks right now. Quite simply, young people in their twenties make up the future of our churches. We need to start seeing them as our future elders, deacons, Sunday school teachers, basically the next generation of Christian leaders.

They need to be trained, equipped, encouraged, discipled, taught and prepared to lead the church well in the years to come. We will miss out on contributing to the future health and vitality of local church congregations if we do not focus intently on helping young adult believers grow in maturity, godliness and responsibility.

But, as you can see from my above comments, it's not just about helping and preparing *them*. It's also about what they can contribute to the life and health of our local congregations right now; it's about *us* as well. It's the young adults in our midst who are often on the "front lines" evangelistically—involved in many social activities and engagements, changing jobs regularly and rubbing shoulders with unbelievers in a multitude of ways.

Because of this, their insights into how we can be better engaging the culture around us with the gospel of Jesus Christ can be invaluable. We need their thoughts, their input and their voices; they are an integral part of the local "body" of Jesus Christ, and we will be richer for engaging, including and listening to them!

The young adults in our church are *ready* to be engaged, served, led and equipped by us.

So, yes, engagement of the millennials in our congregations is about the future health and influence of the church, but it's also about the health and vitality of the church—and its gospel witness and impact in culture—right now. Now is the time to begin incorporating our young people in the very central work and ministry of the church.

What Are They Thinking About?

Before getting into some practical suggestions reaching out to young adults, I want to ask one more "set-up" question: What are they thinking? What is the general mindset of the twentysomethings in our local congregations? What are they looking for from a church? What do they desire to see from the older generations who are leading the church? While I can't speak for every millennial in every local church congregation in our country, I can offer some insights from the conversations and experiences I've had.

First, almost all of the twentysomethings I know in the local church are eager—to varying degrees, of course—to find some kind of discipleship and mentorship in the context of the local church.

They are not leaving our church because they don't want spiritual depth; they are leaving because of a lack of deep community, a place where they can grow personally in their walk with the Lord Jesus Christ.

We have a tremendous opportunity to *disciple career folks who actually want to be discipled!* More often than not, I don't find young adults to be incredibly cynical about the older generation.

In fact, I've heard dozens of twentysomethings in my church and in other contexts speak to their desire to be mentored and discipled by an older man or woman who is further "down the road" in a walk with Jesus, a marriage relationship and the experience of raising children. They're open to leadership and are in a season of life when they are actively looking for godly guidance.

Next, the twentysomethings in the church can offer incredible and invaluable help to the older elders and pastors with regard to insights in reaching the secular culture with the gospel of Jesus Christ. Most of the pastors here spend most of their work weeks in the church building—meeting with people, meeting with each other, preparing sermons and planning ministry services and events.

The career folks are out in the workplace, engaging in social events, hearing interesting conversations . . . all of which makes them equipped to offer key insights to contextualization and cultural engagement to the church leaders.

We have a tremendous opportunity to *learn from our career folks how we can better engage our secular culture with the gospel of Jesus Christ.* In my experience, twentysomethings are extremely excited about engaging alongside their pastors and church leaders in this way.

They want to offer their insights.

They want to be "turned loose" in gospel witness.

They long to be part of the church's "plan" for engaging the culture around them with the gospel of Jesus Christ.

Often, they simply aren't invited into this process and work. Also, the twentysomethings in our church body can—given their work and cultural situations—provide for the local church a front-line evangelistic presence, which can build the overall church body through outreach and invitations.

If we are not nurturing them through providing them some ministry and relational venue to which they would be willing to bring their baby Christian and non-Christian friends, then that is on us, not on them!

If we do find a way to provide a thoroughly biblical and gospel-centered context of ministry here, which also provides non-awkward social engagement and relational community, then there is a good chance that such a community could become a cutting edge evangelistic "arm" for the church.

We have a tremendous opportunity to *benefit and grow as a church through our career folks bringing unbelievers into our church body to hear the gospel and be changed by it.* Many of the young adult believers I know are actually very bold with their friends and co-workers about their faith and are quite willing to invite them to something (an event, meeting, worship service, etc.) that boldly and clearly proclaims the gospel of Jesus Christ explicitly.

But, they have a big "lame" radar, and they will steer clear of inviting friends to anything that smacks of inauthenticity, staleness or simply being "out of touch" with culture and the world today. It's not the gospel of Jesus Christ that they're afraid of; they're willing to confront their peers with this. It's sometimes the invisible "barriers" of our churches, which makes engagement with young adults far more difficult.

**They are looking for a community
in which they can identify a godly spouse.**

Finally, the twentysomethings in our church body, quite simply, should be given the opportunity—and even gently encouraged—to look for godly spouses in the context of the local church. While we should not advertise this as the main focus of a "career ministry," we should not be shy about this desire as church leaders either.

Where else would we counsel our own sons and daughters to begin looking for a godly wife or husband? Would we not want them to consider a spouse from the midst of a gospel-centered and biblical-grounded community in the context of the local church?

We have a tremendous opportunity to *lay the groundwork for a community of career folks—within our local church—to form dating relationships that can lead to godly Christian marriages in the years to come.* A lot of times, I find that young adults are a lot more comfortable talking about their singleness (and their search for a godly husband or wife) than we think they are!

The reality is that most young Christian adults really do see the stupidity of the "bar scene" and the general hopelessness of finding a godly spouse in such a context. They are fairly open about their desire to seek out a godly companion in the context of a church.

It's not wrong for us, as church leaders, to think about intentionally providing a ministry place in the context of our church for connecting young adults who will come together to form godly marriages. Many of them are intentionally looking for such a place!

What I am really trying to say here is this: The young adults in our church are *ready* to be engaged, served, led and equipped by us. They are looking for discipleship relationships with older believers. They are ready to be equipped and sent out for the sake of gospel witness. They want a place—in the context of the local church—where they can invite their unbelieving friends and co-workers. They are looking for a community in which they can identify a godly spouse. Sadly, far too often, we don't engage our young adult members on these fronts. So, let me humbly suggest some ways forward for the church today.

Suggestions for the Church

Reaching and engaging the young adults in our congregations in an intentional and focused way is a huge endeavor. But, as I've argued, we need to be figuring this out in our local churches today. To be clear, I'm mainly speaking to churches that are currently somewhat intergenerational. I'm not necessarily addressing an urban church plant where 90 percent of the people are in their twenties! They probably need to work in the opposite direction in the coming years, for the sake of the inter-generational health and substance of their congregation.

However, I'd like to give suggestions to churches with a solid "older" generation of leaders that also have a significant (although perhaps small) group of young twentysomethings in their congregation. Many such churches, in my immediate experience, are wrestling through how to better connect these young adults to the life and ministry of the church.

Allow me to first lay some methodological and "big picture" groundwork regarding the key assumptions I will make about what a "career ministry" should look like. Here are my beginning assumptions and convictions about such a focused ministry in the context of a local church:

- A career ministry needs to provide a genuine and deep place of *discipleship and training* for twentysomethings who have grown up in the church (our church or others), and who have been walking with Jesus for quite some time. This needs to be a place where a twenty-two-year old could potentially spend eight years and be legitimately discipled, taught the Bible well, challenged in his or her faith and mature as a follower of Jesus Christ.

  In other words, there needs to be substantive Bible teaching and training that will fulfill the appetites of somewhat mature followers of Jesus Christ, or they will become hungry for more "meat" and turn elsewhere for training and teaching.

- A career ministry needs to provide a genuine and comfortable place of *social connections and relational community*. The above—training and teaching—cannot and will not happen without a deep context of relationships and community. Career folks are attending church to learn about God; that is a given. But, they are also going to gravitate toward places where there are people like them—people who share interests and people with whom they can spend time outside of church events. Whatever a career ministry looks like, it must provide a strong, warm and comfortable context for growing relationships in non-awkward social settings.

**A ministry needs a core group
of young people to "champion" it
and drive it forward.**

- A career ministry needs to provide an *accessible and intelligible context for unbelievers* in both its worship and its teaching. This is the difficult, but a necessary, balance that needs to be struck in this kind of church-based ministry. It's the case for at least two reasons.

First, this ministry needs to be a key place in which the church can reach unbelievers with the gospel of Jesus Christ.

Second, this ministry needs to be a place where the career folks are not only comfortable with bringing their unbelieving friends, but are actually eager to do so. This focal point will obviously affect decisions that are made about meeting venue, musical style, dress, event choices, and even language and demeanor in teaching. The goal, of course, is never to "water down" the gospel of Jesus Christ, but to be accessible and intelligible to churched and unchurched people alike.

- A career ministry needs to provide a *clear path and connection to the overall local church body.* While I am going to advocate for a specific ministry devoted to career folks, this does not mean that the intention for such a ministry is to create a church within the church—or certainly a separate congregation outside of the wider, multi-generational congregation here. There needs to be a significant connection with the overall church body and the wider congregation. Again, there are tensions and difficulties here that will need to be examined carefully.

These are my beginning assumptions and convictions with regard to a focused ministry to young adults in the context of a local church. Such a ministry must be biblically and theologically substantive (able to bring young believers in Jesus to higher levels of spiritual maturity).

It must be relationally focused (able to connect people in deep ways to others in the same "season" of life). It must be accessible to the unchurched (a context into which young adults could easily invite unbelieving co-workers).

It must be integrally connected to the overall life of the local congregation (not "its own thing" with a life completely of its own, apart from the wider church body).

How does a church actually move to accomplishing a ministry such as this? Here are four practical ways forward that your church could take:

1. *Identify the right pastoral leadership to oversee this specific ministry commitment to young adults.*

The first step would be to recruit from the outside—or identify from the inside—a dynamic pastoral leader who could legitimately spearhead such an effort and build from the ground up a career ministry in the context of your local church.

This individual needs to share your "DNA"—a commitment to Bible teaching, the proclamation of the gospel and a passion for the lost, for example—but also needs to have a certain dynamism in teaching, as well as leadership gifts in the areas of creativity and innovation.

In a smaller church context, this certainly does not need to be a paid member of the pastoral staff; it simply needs to be a leader who has the relational gifting, leadership skill set and theological training to spearhead the growth and development of a substantive ministry to the young adults in your congregation. With the right leader, or "point person," in place, the young people should find that they have significant spiritual investment and excitement from the leaders of their church.

2. *Form, train and involve a lay leader team of young professionals to help lead and develop this ministry.*

One of the first and most vital steps for this pastoral leader would be to recruit, develop and begin to train a team of dynamic young people around whom the career ministry would be formed. Ideally, there would be developing and growing relational connections within this "team," which could be made up of between ten and twenty male and female "career" folks. Such a ministry needs a core group of young people to "champion" it and drive it forward.

Many local church leaders need to be challenged to stop looking at twentysomethings as simply immature believers.

The first priority of the pastoral or lay leader of such a ministry should be identifying and gathering the key young people in the church who can help build up a ministry to the young adults. This core group must be discipled, trained, encouraged and equipped to begin to invest widely in the church and gather peers for engagement in the wider body. This is a key step!

3. *Identify the best venue for some sort of weekly or monthly gathering of the young adults in the church congregation.*

The next step would be for the pastoral or lay leader—with the support and input of the lay leader team—to identify the right venue for a weekly or monthly gathering of worship and Bible teaching for the career ministry.

The right venue would have the right ambiance for singing and Bible teaching—probably an informal and accessible space with which people in the area would already be somewhat familiar.

The reality is that, for many young adults, ambiance and space are very important! It's not unspiritual to think very carefully about the best gathering space for the young adults when they do gather for age-specific fellowship, teaching and ministry.

Remember, when leadership is committed to building the overall investment and engagement of young adults in the fellowship of the overall church congregation, and the more that such people grow in relationships with each other, the more the church body will be built up.

I would urge church leaders not to be troubled by an "age-specific" gathering, but to see that everyone in the church needs a smaller place—outside of the corporate worship gathering—to connect relationally. The key here is leadership—both pastoral and lay—that are committed to connect the members of such a young adult ministry to the broader congregation.

4. *Determine a context-specific plan for the program and structure of your regular young adult gathering.*

As for the program and structure of the ministry itself, the main worship meeting (singing and Bible teaching) could take place on a Sunday night. (My second choice would be a weeknight.) Members of the ministry would be encouraged to attend corporate worship on either Saturday nights or Sunday mornings and to join a small group, made up of people in the young adult ministry or of members in the wider church body.

The small groups could be career ministry specific but could also be part of the overall church model of small groups (studying the same curriculum, under the oversight of the same pastoral leadership, etc.). The specific structure and program, of course, will depend largely on the church context in which you serve.

Any decisions about this regular gathering can and should be made with significant input from the team of young adult lay leaders that the point person has gathered. The reality is that these lay leaders are going to invest in something if they have been given significant ownership in it. Work with them, and listen to them as you form this ministry commitment!

Because individuals come from many different denominational and church contexts, it won't be helpful to get too much more detailed than I've already gotten in this section.

I do believe, though, that these basic steps in the formation of a young adult ministry can be applied in a variety of situations, contexts and places. In a nutshell, I would encourage all church leaders to consider taking these four steps:

1. Find a pastoral or lay leader who is capable to lead such a ministry effort.
2. Task that leader to gather and equip a team of young adult lay leaders.
3. Identify the right venue for an age-specific gathering or community.
4. Have this group of leaders plan and structure the ministry, giving them significant ownership.

Results

What might the results be if we as local church leaders made a renewed effort to reach, encourage, disciple and equip the young adults/twentysomethings in our midst? First, *they* will be made aware of our love for them and spiritual commitment to them. Even if we make some initial mistakes with regard to structure or venue, our young adults will see the church's spiritual care for them and our desire for them to be vitally involved in the life of the local church congregation.

We will also be enriched, as the twentysomethings in our midst are more actively and intentionally folded into the lives of our churches.

We'll be energized by their passion, as well as their insights for engaging culture with the gospel of Jesus Christ.

We'll be challenged and, yes, sometimes frustrated, by their questioning of certain traditions, which may or may not be tied to firm biblical or theological foundations.

Overall, though, they will broaden our expression of worship and our insights into how to worship God together and to reach the world around us in His name.

And perhaps most importantly, *the church* will be better prepared for years of faithfulness to Jesus Christ and the biblical gospel in the years to come. Many local church leaders need to be challenged to stop looking at twentysomethings as simply immature believers and to start looking at them as the future elders, deacons, teachers and lay leaders of our churches.

They need to be trained, engaged and equipped, even now, to begin contributing to the lives of our churches, for the sake of future faithfulness and witness to the world. Now is the time!

Conclusion

I realize that this chapter has taken a bit of a "turn" from the tone and audience of the rest of the book. That's intentional, because it's my conviction that the issues are connected. Parents, of course, need to be called to raise their children to know Jesus Christ and invest in His church. There can be a "gap", though, as adult children enter their college and post-college years—a gap during which they don't know how to engage with the church (and the church often does little to help them).

This chapter has provided one way for the leadership of local churches to move into this gap, carrying on the work of Christian parents and welcoming young adults into the life of the body of Christ—with specific focus and engagement.

It's my prayer that local churches around this country will continue to grow in their teaching, engagement and gospel-centered training of these young adults who are so key to our congregations' future vitality and gospel witness.

11

The Millennials and the Church

After presenting a general strategy for the engagement of the local church in the lives and hearts of young adults/twentysomethings in its midst, it makes sense to delve a bit deeper into the nature of this "millennial" bunch, examining their issues with the church, their particular values and desires and all of the implications for Christian parents and church leaders that emerge from these observations.

I've come to some quite hopeful conclusions as I've spoken with, discipled and mentored young millennial believers. I'm convinced that there are very bright days ahead for their engagement in the church of Jesus Christ; because of this, I hope this chapter is encouraging and enlightening to you as well!

Who Are They?

People can mean a lot of different things when they talk about the "millennial" generation. Some claim that this generation begins with people who are born in the early 1980s;

others include young people who have even been born after the year 2000.

For the purpose of this chapter, I'm going to define a millennial as someone who was born between 1983 and 1997; or, at the time of the composition of this book, those who are currently between the ages of 18 and 32.

This means I'm including in these observations and conclusions young men and women who are currently college-age, young twentysomethings and also those in their late twenties who are getting married and beginning to have children. It's a wide range of life experience, I know, but people in this age range share some key characteristics and convictions when it comes to Christian faith and the church.

If it seems too "slick" and "canned," they don't want anything to do with it.

Let me make one more clarifying point, here, before we dive into the issues of millennials. I will be discussing specifically millennials who self-identify as "Christian." It wouldn't be helpful to seek to make broad generalizations about every millennial from every religious perspective everywhere! I'm focusing on young men and women, ages eighteen to thirty-two in America who would still call themselves "Christians."

They may or may not be currently involved in a local church or even be going to church. But their convictions have led them to still embrace the Christian faith and generally continue the pursuit of a personal relationship with Jesus Christ.

It's about these millennials that I'll now make some observations, which I think lead to very key conclusions about our
engagement with them for the sake of the gospel of Jesus
Christ, as well as for the sake of His body, the church.

Issues with the Church

I've had hundreds of conversations with millennials about
the church. These conversations happen because, first of all,
I'm a college pastor. This means that, each week, I'm having
probably eight to twelve one-on-one meetings with eigh-
teen- to twenty-two-year-olds, during which we talk about
personal faith, biblical/theological issues and, of course, the
local church.

I'm also currently—by my own definition—part of the
Christian "millennial" group that I've identified in this chapter. So, my peers are also millennials, and we talk about the
church. I'm not saying I'm an expert; I am saying that I'm constantly engaging with millennials about the issues this chapter
addresses.

What I'm going to lay out below are four of the primary
"issues" millennials have with local churches today. They are
issues that have certainly led to over-reactions against church
involvement and engagement; my generation must not be left
"off the hook" for such reactions.

These issues are not excuses for their abandonment of church
membership, service, giving and involvement. Still, they are key
issues for Christian parents and church leaders to be aware of
today. So, what "issues" do millennials raise about the church
today? What frustrates them and causes them to abandon their
engagement with local manifestations of the body of Christ?

The "Authenticity" Issue

"It just seems like people at that church are putting on a front." "Those people act like they have it all together; there's no place for being 'real' there." "Every time that pastor talks, he just seems like a big fake." These are all real comments that I've heard millennials make about churches in our area. They're different, but they're really all the same.

The first issue that millennials raise with the church today is one I'll call the "authenticity" issue, which basically means that they have found many churches to be places that are not "real," however they choose to define that.

They view many churches to be places that are full of "fake" people—people who deny their brokenness, struggle and sin, and try to put on a good face, dress nice on Sundays and repeat the right Christian "catchphrases" to each other each week at church and in small group Bible studies.

Many millennials have come to the conclusion that the local church is not a place for people, then, to actually be "real" and authentic with each other. It's not a place for believers in Jesus to confess sin openly, grieve together, struggle honestly and openly with doubts and help broken people heal.

They crave authentic relationships and interaction and become quickly disillusioned when they see the church as lacking this.

We need to understand, on this point, that no generation has a better "radar" for fake people and inauthentic conversations than the millennial generation. If they get even a whiff of someone who is putting on a show at church—not being "real" with them—they're going to be turned off. The message itself, on a Sunday morning, could be wonderfully powerful and biblically faithful; if it's presented as a "show," or with too much self-consciousness, it will be quickly dismissed.

Now, this first issue that the millennials raise is, of course, not a valid one in every case. Millennials have been guilty of calling very authentic Christians "fake" if they sense a lack of authenticity; many times those accusations are far too quickly tossed.

> Many millennials grow frustrated
> when they see the local church become
> a "holy huddle"—mindful only
> of its own affairs.

Nevertheless, we need to know and understand the way that twentysomethings crave authentic spiritual relationships and conversations in the body of Christ, and why they react in a strongly negative way when they sense people just "going through the motions" at church or see a church that is seeking to "put on a show." They want honesty, and they want real people who are seeking—and sometimes struggling with—a relationship with a real God. More on this later.

The "Service" Issue

Just a few years ago, a group of college students left a solid local church in our town, which they had been attending for a couple of years, to get involved at a start-up church plant down the street. Their main reason? Well, as they expressed it to their former pastor, they were drawn to the new church's monthly commitment to service in the community as a congregation.

One Sunday each month, they actually did not meet for corporate worship, but they went out together as a church body to do a service or work project somewhere in the local area. This resonated with these college students so much that they were drawn to the service of this new church.

As you can tell, I'm not talking about the worship service here, but the way that the church is engaged in service to others—outside the "walls" of its local congregation. Larry Osborne, the pastor of North Coast Church in Northern California, has sometimes referred to this area of focus from millennials as the "Bono Factor."[1]

In other words, it's the question from the millennials to the local church that goes something like this: "What are you doing for others? What are you doing to serve the world around you in the name of Christ?" Cultural leaders and influencers, like Bono, have had a huge influence on the way that millennials think about the importance of using a platform or position for the good of the world; they resonate with the way that such leaders have embraced certain causes and championed them for the sake of justice, peace and healing.

They want to know whether the local church is only turned inward, or if it is engaged in service, justice and healing for the wider world.

Here, again, on this point, the accusations against the church can sometimes be issued too quickly. Many local churches are indeed engaged in service to their community, and they are also involved in helping and supporting causes for the sake of God's people around the world.

Often, the "service" commitments of any given local church will not be readily obvious to those who simply attend each week for corporate worship; so, young people might conclude that "all the church does" is gather together and think about itself. Many times, this is not fair, or even accurate.

Still, it is important for church leaders to understand this concern from millennials that God's people be turned "outward," as well as "inward." They long to see the church serving the world in the name of Jesus in vibrant ways. They want to understand the way the gospel of Jesus Christ shapes personal and private convictions, as well as public involvement and engagement for the glory of God.

The "Attractional" Issue

One male millennial told me recently: "I really have no interest in the 'praise band' thing in church. That seems to appeal to some people, but that's not going to get me excited." He happened to be a young man with wonderful musical gifts, and he was also a bit of a musical elitist! Still, his comment betrayed some of the waning enthusiasm among millennials toward the factors that were drawing people to more contemporary churches in past decades.

Millennials, largely, seem to be getting turned off by the "attractional" approach to church, embraced by so many of the mega-churches during the church growth movement of the 1990s and the early 2000s.

Some millennials, of course, have grown up in large evangelical churches that are part of this movement; they are growing cynical about anything that resembles a "performance" when it comes to the corporate gathering of worship for God's people. To put it quite simply, if it seems too "slick" and "canned," they don't want anything to do with it.

Many of the approaches of the "attractional" church model fall into the category of "fake" or "sales pitch" in the eyes of young millennials. They don't want to be bought with coffee, loud music or stylishly casual pastors. They resist being "attracted"; they want to be engaged with the true gospel of Jesus Christ . . . if it is indeed the eternal good news of the real God.

The "Silo" Issue

In one conversation with a twenty-five-year old millennial, I quickly observed that his "catchphrase" for the church seemed to be "out of touch." While still self-identifying as a Christian, and a follower of Jesus Christ, this young man had significantly distanced himself from the local church for a period of about two years, and he was explaining this to me. His honesty was refreshing and helpful for me, and I told him so.

Again and again, he expressed frustration at the ways that each church that he had attended throughout college seemed blissfully ignorant of the real issues at hand in the culture today. They met week after week for worship, as if they were in their own little world—almost living on a different planet from the rest of the people in their town and surrounding culture.

This came to a head, for this young person, when the church he was attending gathered for worship on a Sunday following a significant national tragedy . . . and no mention was made of the tragedy at all in the corporate worship service, even in the prayer. Things just went on as planned, and he saw this as shocking, given the events of the previous week.

This young millennial had described perfectly the fourth significant issue that his generation has with the local church: the "silo" mentality. Many millennials grow frustrated when they see the local church become a "holy huddle"—mindful only of its own affairs (which are sometimes messy in their own right!). They see many churches as providing only a safe "silo" for Christians, who refuse to engage with the "real" issues in the culture that are at hand because they are frightened, confused or simply ignorant.

They want to see how Christianity is rooted in the traditions of the past.

Now, again, there are many unfair accusations that are thrown here by millennials. We might reply to their frustrations, for example, that the primary purpose of the weekly gathering of corporate worship for God's people in the local church is not to "engage culture," but to worship God according to His Word.

Still, a community that displays no awareness of what is going on in the world—both locally and globally—is going to be a community that is quickly written off by millennials as "irrelevant." We need to be aware of this critique.

Non-Issues with the Church

So, I've identified and explained, above, four of the major "issues" that millennials seem to have with the church today. It's not an exhaustive list, but I think it helps us identify the general mindset of this generation, which is now making up the young adults and twentysomethings in our local church congregations. We need to work hard to understand what they are thinking—their perceptions, frustrations and desires—in order to better reach them and encourage them in the context of our churches.

Now, I want to go the opposite direction, based on my conversations with millennials (as well as on some recent research and writing about this generation). I want to invite you to explore with me some "non-issues" for millennials with regard to the local church.

To put this a different way, I want to explain how some of the assumed roadblocks to church involvement from the millennials' parents' generation can no longer be assumed to be roadblocks for millennials. So, what are some of these "non-issues" for millennials, when it comes to their view of the local church?

The "Otherness" of Church

This point, really, is the other side of the issue that millennials have with the "attractional" church model, which often strikes them as far too rehearsed, slick and canned (and sometimes shallow).

Let me explain how I've put together some of the conversations and experiences I've had with millennials about this "non-issue."

The generation of parents who have raised millennials (those now in their forties and fifties) were drawn to churches that fully embraced the church growth movement and strategy, which was led and fueled in a major way by Bill Hybels and Willow Creek Community Church outside of Chicago.[2]

If I could drastically over-simplify the strategy of this movement, it was basically about making the church "experience" resemble the familiar forms of culture more closely, without losing the substance of biblical teaching and the gospel of Jesus Christ.

So, when young adults twenty years ago—many of whom had grown somewhat disillusioned with "stiff," "formal" and "fake" traditional churches—walked into a church service that felt like either a rock concert or a coffee shop, they embraced it as a new way of doing church. It was more casual, more welcoming and an easier place to both worship and invite unbelieving friends and neighbors.

Many of the assumed "roadblocks" to church had been removed; church seemed more like a natural extension of the rest of their lives, rather than a strange weekly experience that was decades behind culture in numerous ways.

I would argue that millennials are not struggling with the "otherness" of church nearly as much as their parents were, if they are even struggling with it at all.

In fact, I would go one step further to argue that, when millennials do decide to seek God, biblical teaching and the church, they are actually *after* something that looks drastically different than their culture, rather than something that tries to resemble it.

Millennials are engaged in the pursuit of the real, and if they do attend church, it is because they are desperately seeking a God who is transcendent. Because of this, they expect church to be "different" than their culture; they'll be disappointed if it's not. They want to see how Christianity is rooted in the traditions of the past. They're not opposed to singing the words of hymns that were penned by believers who lived hundreds of years ago. I shared this insight (millennials craving the "otherness" and sacredness of church) with a focus group of ten twenty-one- to twenty-two-year-olds this past year, and they all enthusiastically agreed with it.

To put it in a different way, millennials don't attend church to be entertained, or to relax; they can go to a real rock concert or a real coffee shop if they want to do that. They're comfortable with the "otherness" of the church; they expect it and perhaps even demand it.

Millennials are drawn to real fellowship—real unity around the Gospel of Jesus Christ.

The Offense of the Gospel

The catchphrase for many of the mega-churches that emerged out of the church growth movement of the 1990s was "seeker sensitive." That's not a bad phrase, or approach, in and of itself. I would hope that no local church would want to self-identify as "seeker *insensitive!*"

However, my conviction is that many of the seeker-sensitive churches went a step too far—a step past being sensitive only to seekers. They actually began attempting to be seeker sensitive and also "cynic sensitive." Let me explain what I mean.

A genuine "seeker" (someone who is earnestly and honestly trying to understand who God is, what the Bible teaches and how they can follow Jesus Christ) wants the full message of the gospel—with all of its beauty, power and even offense. A "cynic," however, may be more easily turned off by the offensive aspects of Scripture and the biblical gospel, such as human depravity, the wrath of God, the reality of hell or the exclusivity of Christ.

The way that many large "attractional" churches started to "water down" some of their teaching, in my view, came from a desire to appeal to people who were not actually genuine "seekers," but cynics, when it came to the gospel of Jesus Christ. Many of these churches didn't abandon the biblical gospel; yet, they sought to take some of the immediate "offense" out of it.

I remember a conversation with a twenty-four-year old young man, for example, in which I shared the gospel very explicitly with him. He was not a professing believer, but after the conversation, he thanked me for being so direct. He told me that he appreciated so much that I didn't try to sugarcoat the message of the gospel, and he left thanking me for respecting him enough to tell him what I really thought the Bible taught about sin, the cross, death and heaven and hell.

Millennials who are genuinely seeking to understand the Bible and the gospel of Jesus Christ want the real thing—in all of its power, strangeness (in the eyes of the world) and offense.

They are offended not by church leaders seeking to engage them with the real teaching of the Bible but, rather, by pastors and preachers trying to make the gospel more appealing to them by skipping over the difficult parts (the seriousness of sin, the just wrath of God, etc.). If they're going to fully embrace the gospel and join with the body of Christ in the context of the local church, it's going to be because they get the "real" thing, after wrestling and engaging honestly with Scripture's teaching.

The Richness and Depth of Biblical and Theological Teaching

This "non-issue" follows from the last one (the offense of the gospel). Millennials, largely, seem to really crave the depth and richness of biblical teaching, even when it comes with difficult and complex theology.

They are comfortable wrestling with the tensions of Scripture, and even the apparent contradictions (in fact, sometimes, the tensions and mysteries of Scripture even help convince them of the divine inspiration of Scripture).

The depth and richness of the theology of the Christian faith is not a "turn off" to millennials; it's an appealing strength of a rich faith that is "other" than us.

It's important to see that this idea is a bit of a reversal of the common thinking of many of the churches who fully embraced the assumptions of the church growth movement of the previous decades.

Many such churches, seeing overly complex and confusing theological teaching as problematic for seekers, sought to simplify their messages and teachings, making them more and more practical, accessible and relevant. Now, it's not that millennials don't want practical biblical application and teaching that is relevant to life.

But, they do seem to react negatively to teaching that seems to be all practical "advice," without a commitment to honestly digging into the biblical text, wrestling with the sometimes difficult theological teaching that may be contained therein.

Messages that seem too "canned," with little honest and deep engagement with the biblical text, will not go over well with millennials. They don't want to "skate over the surface" of what the Bible teaches; they want to dive in!

The Reality of Christian Fellowship

It's become my conviction that this final "non-issue" for millennials may become the church's biggest open door to reaching, engaging, training and equipping this generation of young adults in our churches today. This generation, in a far deeper way than the generation of its parents, craves deep and authentic fellowship with God, and with the people of God.

Not only do millennials love and seek true and biblical *koinonia* fellowship, but we all need it and crave it as well!

The biblical term for this is *koinonia*—the fellowship of believers in Jesus Christ, which is formed through genuine fellowship with God the Father, God the Son and God the Holy Spirit. It's the fellowship that is modeled after the deep fellowship of the three-person Godhead itself!

Millennials are drawn to real fellowship—real unity around the gospel of Jesus Christ, which is deeper and stronger than any fellowship the world offers today. Why is this? What is so powerful about genuine Christian fellowship in the eyes of millennials? Millennials have come of age during a twenty-year period of absolutely staggering technological development. They have grown up with e-mail, cell phones, Facebook, Twitter, Instagram and more—all communicative luxuries that their parents probably didn't even dream of!

With these developments, though, many of the millennial generation have grown up in constant social "contact" with other people, without really experiencing the formation of deep and lasting relationships. A texting "conversation" often takes the place of a face-to-face meeting over coffee.

Millennials "tweet" at each other, often without really knowing anything of depth about the people they contact through social media. Sadly, many of us in ministry have seen a troubling lack of deep relationships between even the most tech savvy millennials (and sometimes *especially* among the tech savvy types).

Additionally, the gospel-centered fellowship and relationship between believers in Jesus Christ who are immensely different from one another can be a hugely powerful message to millennials.

Church congregations that include diverse people—whether different races, ages, socioeconomic categories, professions or something else—can be a huge testimony to them about the unifying power of the gospel of Jesus Christ.

Millennials are drawn to a diverse community of drastically different kinds of people who worship a common Savior and affirm the truth and authority of the Word of God.

Millennials also, as noted earlier, have a very strong "fake" radar; they demand authenticity and will run in the other direction from a church that they think lacks it. No matter how cynical a millennial may be about a given church's corporate worship service, if they are drawn into the deep fellowship of the leaders and lay people in the congregation, they can and will find a home there.

Millennials will "put up" with music that feels a bit out of touch if they have come to know the people who lead the music—if they have seen their vibrant love for Jesus, their witness for the gospel and their selfless service to others in the community. (It doesn't hurt if they've been in their home for a nice meal, too!)

Quite often, we've seen relationships—the *koinonia* fellowship of the body of believers—to be the key factor in bringing millennials "back" into community with both Jesus Christ and a local gathering of his people in the church.

Conclusion

There is much I could say here in terms of the conclusions we might draw from these observations. First, let me call all of us—pastors, church leaders, parents—to a posture of humility as we seek to both reach and encourage the millennials in our midst. We need to commit to listening to them and truly hearing them; many of them are cynical and frustrated about the Christian faith and about the local church for valid reasons.

We do have much to learn from them as we consider how we can better build up the body of Christ and reach the world in witness for Him. Even the millennial who is issuing the most unfair critiques of the church probably has a few valid points that would be worth considering!

Also, let me encourage all Christians and church leaders to look first to the true, powerful, biblical gospel as our only "strategy" for reaching and building up millennials in our midst. Let's commit to abandoning gimmicks—trying to "attract" them in new and exciting ways.

Those whom the Lord is drawing to Him, for the sake of using them for His glory and witness in the world, will be drawn by the true, full message of Jesus Christ—His death, resurrection and reign—as is communicated to us in the pages of Scripture. People from every generation, including the millennial generation, need to be changed and motivated by the pure and unadulterated gospel.

Let us all commit to intentionally building relational bridges—in the context of local church life—between the different generations that make up the body of Christ. Not only do millennials love and seek true and biblical *koinonia* fellowship, but we all need it and crave it as well!

Let's commit together to helping make our local churches places of worship, witness and deep and authentic fellowship together, as we stand together in the gospel of Jesus Christ and are built up together under His headship.

12

To Those Who Are Mourning

Let me begin this chapter by saying that if you are the parent of a college-age or young adult child who has walked away from the church, and you've made it to this point in this book, I commend you, and thank you for your patience and commitment.

Reading the first chapters—on the biblical principles of parenting that I laid down—could not have been easy for you. I do not doubt that these chapters brought up sweet memories of the younger days for your child, as well as bitter and stabbing pain when you considered the spiritual state of your son or daughter today. You are among those who carry around a constant burden with you each day—a steady ache that never completely subsides.

The apostle John once wrote: "I have no greater joy than to hear that my children are walking in the truth" (3 John 4). I would argue (and parents of wandering children would agree) that the converse of this statement is equally and powerfully true: There is no greater spiritual pain for a Christian parent than to know that one's child is *not* walking in the truth of the gospel of Jesus Christ.

It's a pain that haunts you every day. You're reminded of it every time another parent of adult children tells you about their son the pastor, their daughter the missionary or their grandkids who are memorizing Scripture and singing in the children's choir at church.

Parents of young adult children who have abandoned the church (at least for now), this chapter is written to you. This will not be intended to "solve" anything, but to help you direct your thoughts, prayers, actions and attitudes toward your children in a biblically faithful and God-honoring way. God hears you. He loves you. And He offers you hope and rest in Him.

Different Stories

In my experience talking with parents whose adult children have abandoned faith in Jesus Christ, as well as talking to those children themselves, there really are no two exactly identical stories. Some would like to suggest that all such young adults take the same path out of the church, but that's simply not the case. Still, there does seem to be some general factors that contribute to the departure of young people from the body of Christ and a public confession of faith in Him.

Let me briefly describe a few of the common "stories" that we hear in our context.

A Slow Fade

The story of the "slow fade" is one of the young person who grows up in the church and—during junior high and high school years—shows no real resistance to the Christian faith, the Gospel and a commitment to Jesus Christ. There's no fighting with parents here, no intellectual objections to gospel faith and no outright rebellion and sin. But, there's also no evidence of a vibrant and personal faith in Jesus Christ that leads to discipleship, obedience and bold witness for the gospel.

He alone can change sinful hearts and mold them to His will.

Christian parents of teens in this state sometimes wonder about the genuineness of their faith, but they comfort themselves in the fact that their son or daughter goes willingly to church and youth group and doesn't seem to have any objections to the Christian faith.

A young woman in our church congregation (I'll call her "Cassie") was a classic example of this. I served as her high school pastor for three years. She was always at youth group, involved in small groups, participated in mission trips and had a close group of friends at church.

However, she never seemed to stand on her own in faith. I got the sense that she was there because it was a social "safe place" for her, rather than because she was really interested in growing in her faith in Jesus Christ. Sadly, during the past few years, my suspicions were confirmed. Finding a new social network during college, she walked away from the church, and from her faith in Jesus.

Even though the boxes were checked during high school, there was no personal relationship with Jesus; that reality was slowly and gradually exposed as she left the familiar community of her church.

Usually, though, the "fade" for such a young person begins during the college years. He or she now lives apart from parents and has the choice to attend church or not. Without any dramatic event, outright sinful behavior or violent fight with parents, a commitment to the local church and the Christian faith just simply . . . fades away.

At some point, usually, the young adult child admits to his or her parents that he or she "doesn't really believe" the claims of the Christian faith any more. The "slow fade" young adult child usually isn't interested in fighting about it; he or she just wants to be left alone. Often, Christian parents are left at a loss, not knowing what to do, or how to engage with their children.

A Sin Issue

Then, there's another story—the "sin issue" story. In this all-too-common tale, a young person grows up in the church, perhaps voluntarily participates in youth group and ministry activities and even exhibits what seems to be a personal relationship with Jesus Christ.

Often, there even seems to be a genuine love for the church—for both learning about the Bible and spending time in fellowship with God's people.

But, a particular preference for sin enters in at some point. In our context, we've seen several different examples of this.

For some, it's a love for partying and binge drinking—an experience that begins in college and opens a whole new door of excitement, pleasure and thrills.

For others, it's a discovery of sexual activity—either in the context of a "committed" relationship, or in more short-term "hook-ups."

For still others, it's a same-sex attraction that is now acted upon for the first time, leading to newfound feelings of belonging and intimacy.

Whatever the particular sin of choice, this sin becomes the touchstone for either a gradual (and sometimes sudden) abandonment of both the Christian faith and involvement in the local church.

The choice is subtly or boldly made—a preference for personal sin over and above a commitment to Jesus Christ and His call to holiness and obedience.

In such cases, it is never a purely intellectual objection to the Christian faith that leads to an abandonment of Jesus Christ and His body, although quite often, young adults with this "story" will mask their departure with such an objection.

It's the preference for sin—a commitment to ungodly behavior—that forces a shift in belief, thinking and theology. This is how it always happens; behavior shifts, and theology must change to match up with it.

Recently, in our community, we've seen more than one student choose first to embrace homosexual relationships and then gradually mold a theology and system of beliefs that will fit in with that lifestyle choice.

Again, the preference for sin (in this case, a sexual relationship with a member of the same sex) forces a change in theology, beliefs and church involvement.

An Angry Reaction

Still other young adults who grow up in the church have some "trigger" that leads them to an angry and violent reaction against the Christian faith and followers of Jesus Christ. In this case, it's not a "slow fade," but a sudden and striking reaction; it's not a preference for a particular sin, per se, but a knee-jerk pushback to something about the church that has hurt or wounded them severely.

This angry reaction could come from something as seemingly small as rejection by one's peers at the youth group at church. It could be a perception that a Christian leader in the congregation has judged them or treated them unfairly. Many times, sadly, this can happen as a result of a major moral failing on the part of a trusted spiritual leader or mentor.

Never cease appealing to God,
begging Him to work in your child's life
by the power of His Holy Spirit.

The reaction, whatever the trigger, is the same: an angry and bitter turning away from the church, which is now identified as a place of judgmental, unwelcoming and hypocritical people.

One young woman with whom I talked cited her treatment from peers during her junior high years as the big "turn off" for her from church. She didn't have a problem with the Bible, Christian theology or Jesus Christ; she had simply been very deeply hurt by Christians who had made her feel left out, lonely and different. For her, if that was how you were treated in the church, then she wanted no part of it.

You can identify the "angry reaction" story, usually, by just asking a few simple questions of a young adult who has abandoned the church with this mentality. If you talk to the "slow fade" young adult, you'll get half-hearted and apathetic responses; he or she won't have much interest in engaging with you.

If you bring up the church to the "angry reaction" young adult, and ask a few pointed questions, you'll see the anger in the eyes very quickly. Before long, you'll be hearing a long list of ways that the church is flawed—and even dangerous. There will be a certain intensity to the conversation, and you'll get the sense that there is something deeply personal in what is being communicated.

A Replacement

The final "story" that we tend to see with young adults in our context who abandon the faith and the local church is the "replacement" story. That is, a commitment to Jesus Christ and His church is "replaced" by a passionate commitment to a certain cause, social concern or even religious movement.

Certainly, such a "replacement" calls into question the validity of the young person's original "commitment" to Jesus Christ. (This is not the place to discuss the doctrine of eternal security; I've done that a bit in the opening chapters of the book.) But, for whatever reason, such a person—in this "story"—becomes enraptured with a life commitment that is something *other* than the gospel of Jesus Christ and the people of God.

Sometimes, such a replacement can happen when young people emerge from a church context that—after being exposed to a community more concerned with social issues, for example—can be seen as a bit "sheltered" or "out of touch" with culture.

They begin to then be disillusioned with the lack of engagement from the church in the "real" issues of society and culture and want to be more on the "frontlines" in fighting AIDS, poverty or social injustices.

Of course, the gospel of Jesus Christ doesn't need to be abandoned in order for someone to engage in these types of causes; I would argue that they are actually natural entailments of the gospel of Jesus Christ for those who follow Him! But, in this "story," young people choose to turn away from a local church for the purpose of championing a certain cause.

One couple I know is extremely excited about their daughter's involvement in the Peace Corps. She is doing wonderful work helping people around the world; yet, they are very honest about their questions concerning her spiritual condition and her devotion to Jesus Christ. She's gone after global "issues" but seems to have abandoned a commitment to the gospel, as well as the personal obedience that accompanies the lives of those who live for God.

Words of Correction

Parents, I don't know what "story" you have experienced with your child. It might be one of the four I've described above. It might be a combination of two or more of them. It might be none of them. Whatever it has looked like, I am sure that it has brought you to your knees. You've mourned your child's chosen departure from Christ and the church. You've wept over the choices of your son or daughter. You may be mourning and weeping even as you read through this book.

With the utmost sincerity and sensitivity to your experience—whatever that looks like—I want to, at this point, offer some gentle "correctives" to you, as you continue to engage with your adult child, pray for him or her and hope for a return to both Jesus Christ and the body of believers in a local church.

Some of these you will already know; yet, you may need to gently remind yourself of their importance. I offer these prayerfully, gently and carefully to you as mourning parents, who long for your children to embrace Jesus and His church.

It Never Depended Solely on You

It's my conviction that, as you continue to process the present spiritual state of your young adult child, you need to start theologically, by recognizing the fundamental priority of God's role in the salvation of any human being.

To put it simply, salvation is a miraculous work of God's Holy Spirit illuminating the mind and heart of an unbeliever; the salvation of your child *never* depended solely on you. Whether or not your child repents of sin and turns to Christ in saving faith is first and foremost God's business. He alone can change sinful hearts and mold them to His will.

Read these familiar words, which speak to the truth of what we're discussing here.

> And you were dead in the trespasses and sins in which you once walked, following the course of this world, following the prince of the power of the air, the spirit that is now at work in the sons of disobedience—among

whom we all once lived in the passions of our flesh, carrying out the desires of the body and the mind, and were by nature children of wrath, like the rest of mankind. But God, being rich in mercy, because of the great love with which he loved us, even when we were dead in our trespasses, made us alive together with Christ—by grace you have been saved—and raised us up with him and seated us with him in the heavenly places in Christ Jesus. (Eph. 2:1-6)

Familiar words, yes. But this passage powerfully reminds us of our natural state apart from Christ Jesus. Every human being born into this world is "dead" in sin, following Satan's rule, and under the resulting just "wrath" of God.

Never quit asking the Author of Salvation to work His miracle of faith in the heart and soul of your child.

Salvation, as one preacher put it, is not about "turning over a new leaf," but about "resurrecting a dead tree!"[1] The only way that salvation—new spiritual life—can happen is if God chooses to make a dead soul "come alive" into faith in Jesus Christ. God is the author of salvation . . . not us.

Parents, remember that even the best mom and dad in the world cannot raise a "dead" soul from the grave! Yes, our job is to bear witness to the one who can do this saving work; we'll talk more about this in a moment. But, that resurrection regenerating work does not depend on us. It never did.

Repent of Sin, not Weakness

In light of this reality (the salvation of our children not finally depending on us), I want to address the question of how—and of what—you are to personally repent for your role in your child's current abandonment of the Christian faith and the Christian church.

You have, no doubt, wrestled and struggled with feelings of guilt, shame, regret and even blame, as you have seen your adult child walk away from the church. How do *you* process this, personally, in your prayers and times with God? To what extent do you allow the weight of your child's departure from active faith sit on you . . . and confess your part in this to God?

First, let me suggest that there may, indeed, be some repentance that needs to happen, as you look back on the years of raising your child in your home. For every single Christian parent, there is some sin—some failure—involved in the raising of children.

Even the best and most sanctified parents sometimes lose their temper, make rash disciplinary decisions or fail to rebuke and teach with enough biblical depth and power. (You can add your own personal failures to that list!)

It is good and right for you to—during this season—look back and repent of the ways that you have not done as well as you might have done in pointing your children to Jesus, teaching them the biblical gospel and setting before them a godly example of the Christian life in every way.

I would also remind you that there are some "failures" in parenting that do not demand repentance—at least in the same way as blatant sins do. I'm talking about the failures of our weakness—our human frailty and inability to act in all perfection and godliness (even when we are serving God faithfully, by the power of his Holy Spirit). This is why I've titled this little section: "Repent of Sin, not Weakness."

Our sins in parenting must indeed be brought to the Lord in prayer; we must beg for His forgiveness and mercy—at the cross—for the ways we have failed as parents. But, we must also remember that we are all weak, frail . . . and human.

As I have tried to remind you before, you were never the one who was called to "convert" your child or serve as God, Lord or Savior to them; none of us is capable of this kind of responsibility! So, repent of sin. But, don't feel sorry for your weakness.

Don't heap guilt on yourself for being weak, human and unable to make the heart of your child spiritually "come alive" to faith in Jesus. That was always God's role; it was a burden too heavy for a weak human being to carry.

Remember God's Love for Your Child

I'll now say something to you, which I know you probably have already repeated to yourself dozens and dozens (maybe hundreds) of times: God's love for your child is deeper, stronger and fuller that yours could ever be. God is your child's Creator; He knows his or her heart—in all of its sin, doubts, fears and depth.

Listen to those well-known verses from Psalm 139, as King David considers God's knowledge and love of him.

> For you formed my inward parts;
>   you knitted me together in my mother's womb.
> I praise you, for I am fearfully and wonderfully made.

Wonderful are your works;
  my soul knows it very well.
My frame was not hidden from you,
when I was being made in secret,
  intricately woven in the depths of the earth.
Your eyes saw my unformed substance;
in your book were written, every one of them,
  the days that were formed for me,
  when as yet there was none of them.

(Ps. 139:13–16)

There has not been one day of your child's life that has not been carefully and strategically designed by God, the Creator. He knew your child long before he or she was born. The struggles and sins of your child are not hidden from your God.

However much you intensely feel—and even ache—with love and care for your child . . . God loves and cares even more. The pain that you feel because of your child's broken relationship with God is known by your God. And there is no one in the universe who loves your child more than your child's Maker.

Never Stop Praying

Finally, let me just offer a simple, but essential, reminder that the absolute best eternally-minded and spiritually effective action you can keep taking on behalf of your child is approaching God in prayer on his or her behalf. Don't give up on prayer.

Never cease appealing to God, begging Him to work in your child's life by the power of His Holy Spirit. Keep on asking God to do what you can't do: transform the heart and soul of your adult child and lead him or her to repentance of sin, faith in Jesus and love for God's Word and God's people.

To borrow a phrase from Winston Churchill on this point: Don't ever, ever, ever give up on praying for your child.[2] This commitment to steady and constant prayer will accomplish a few things in your heart, as well as, Lord willing, bring about change in the life of your child.

He knows your pain. He hears your prayers. He longs for you.

First, it will remind you of your total reliance and dependence on God to bring about the desired change in your child's heart and life; it will force you to remember that God alone is the one who can bring repentance and faith.

Second, it will strengthen your own relationship with God, rather than embittering you against your Savior. As you spend time reading the Word, responding to God in prayer and petitioning him on your child's behalf, I assure you that you will be strengthened in your faith and your own love for Jesus.

Don't stop praying. Don't stop trusting your God. Never quit asking the Author of Salvation to work His miracle of faith in the heart and soul of your child.

Words of Hope

Let me end by offering a few words of hope. The first word is anecdotal. The second is theological. The final word is personal.

Recently, several dear friends of ours have seen adult children, who had strayed quite far from Christ and the church, begin to return to both a personal commitment to Jesus and involvement in the body of believers. Each situation has been different; one young man has been utterly broken by the abandonment of his wife of just three years and has turned to God for help, strength and meaning. I am praying that he will find his joy, strength and peace in Jesus Christ, and he seems very open to this.

Another young man has been re-awakened to the need for a spiritual life and purpose through the unexpected gift of children (who came along sooner than he and his young wife had planned!).

He is now coming to church regularly, seeking to "re-discover" the centrality of the gospel, as he wants to lead his family well under the rule of God's Word.

Here's the point: It's not over. The story is not over yet. We've seen adult children captured by the seriousness of sin, which forces them to turn back to the God of grace they once confessed.

Second, a theological word. God has promised that His Word—when it goes out from Him—will not return to Him "empty"(see Isa. 55:11). Certainly, God's Word and truth can be sinfully rejected; people do this all the time. But, God's Word is indeed powerful and effective. Young adults who have been exposed to it for years and years cannot help but be affected by it.

Even after years and years of hardening, the foundation of gospel proclamation and biblical teaching can still "break through" to their hearts and minds. God's Word is that powerful, that effective. Don't doubt the power of God's Word, even as it was proclaimed to your children years ago!

Third, a personal word; if you are indeed in Christ, remember that God loves you dearly, strongly and passionately. He is your heavenly Father, and you are His treasured possession . . . His joy. He knows your pain. He hears your prayers. He longs for you to trust Him more and love Him more deeply—even as you cry out to Him on behalf of your child.

Never forget that, amid the pain of seeing your child wander from God and His people, your own worship of God and love for His Son are your priority. Find your peace—your deepest joy—in your God. He, after all, is the Christian's treasure, joy and crown. Even as you sometimes weep, ask God to help you daily say to Him: "You are my Lord; / I have no good apart from you" (Ps. 16:2).

13

To the Kids

If you're reading this final chapter, and have made it through the entire book, then, first, let me say "thank you." You're most likely a future parent, current parent, pastor or ministry leader who is wrestling through questions about how to better reach, equip and disciple young people toward years of worship to Jesus and service and involvement in His church.

While this chapter is the first one in this book not addressed directly to you, I hope that you read it, engage with it and perhaps pass it along to young adults in your context who might benefit from it. If you're a college student or young adult, then this chapter is specifically and directly for you. In fact, it's the only chapter in this book that I have written not *about* you, but *to* you.

I want to talk to you about your relationship with Jesus Christ and, in relation to that, your level of involvement and service in the local church. My goal is to be frank, honest and open with you. Some of you may be cynical toward the

Christian faith and the church. Some of you may be "on the fence" with regard to the future of your engagement with God's people.

Others of you may be committed to Jesus Christ, but wrestling with what your "adult" engagement with the body of Christ will look like. What follows in this chapter are my words to you.

I offer them with love, prayers, hope and humility . . . for God's glory in your hearts and lives.

Your Parents

Let me begin by talking to you about your parents. If you were raised in a generally Christian home, then probably your parents were the most immediate and formative influence on your early Christian life, learning and development. This can be a good thing; perhaps for you it was a troubling thing!

Let me make just two suggestions for you, as you process your relationship with your parents and its connection to your current walk with the Lord Jesus Christ and relationship with His people in the context of the church.

Imperfect People

Let's get something very clearly out on the table, right at the outset: Your parents are imperfect and sinful people. I don't know them, but I know—according to the Bible—that this is true of them. It probably would not be difficult for you to sit down right now and come up with a very full list of the faults of your parents.

You could describe their sinful tendencies, their weaknesses, their failures, their mistakes and, of course, the ways that they frustrated you endlessly with their choices, person-alities or quirks. You know, better than anyone else, that your parents are imperfect people!

The Bible, in fact, is very clear that even Christians will not be made perfect until they are in heaven with Jesus—living with glorified bodies and minds and hearts that are finally free from the influence of sin.

Although redeemed and forgiven by the sacrificial death and resurrection of Jesus, followers of Him still wrestle with their sinful tendencies and weaknesses, although they should be gradually becoming more and more holy, godly and like Jesus their Savior.

Jesus wants to one day present the church as forever holy and perfect. The church is something Jesus Christ . . . loves dearly.

Here's the danger you need to work to avoid, when it comes to the imperfections, weaknesses and even the sins of your parents: the tendency to grow cynical and bitter toward the church, and even toward Jesus Christ, *because* of your parents' failures and imperfections.

Far too many young adults have lumped their entire view of Scripture and the gospel in with their frustrations with their Christian parents . . . and have grown disillusioned with the whole package of commitment to Jesus Christ and His people.

I'll say more on this in a moment, but for now, let me just strongly say this: *Your parents' imperfections and weaknesses should not be the reason that you walk away from a perfect and gloriously strong Savior.*

Honor, not Imitation

So, what do you do about your parents? More specifically, what do you do about parents whom you feel have hurt you, wounded you or damaged your picture of Christian faith and the church of Jesus Christ in some way?

Here is some good news: The call to follow Jesus Christ is not synonymous with a call to imitate your parents! You don't have to be just like them; in fact, there are probably ways that you—given the way God has particularly and uniquely created you—are called to be *not* like them.

You see, for far too many young people, a relationship with Jesus Christ (and often a relationship with the church as well) has become too intrinsically wrapped up with a relationship with parents. And, quite often, relationships with parents can be difficult—filled with tension, disagreement, pain and, yes, sin. The fact is that even the most healthy parent-child relationships are going to be affected by the results of the fall in all of our lives and hearts.

What I'm suggesting here is that you need to work to intentionally "separate" your relationship with Jesus Christ and involvement in His church from your relationship with your parents. You are not called to be exactly like your parents; you *are* called to follow Jesus and to more and more resemble Him.

Following Jesus and joining His body, the church, does not need to be deeply wrapped up in the faith of your parents. It needs to be about you and God.

Here's the catch, though, with regard to your parents (if you are truly seeking to honor Jesus as you relate to them): You are called to honor them.

What does this mean? Again, it's not about imitation; honoring your parents doesn't mean "agreeing" with everything they have done, or even liking all of the aspects of the way they live their lives and relate to God and the church.

But, still, there is this call to "honor" them—it's one of the Ten Commandments, which you may remember from your Sunday school days! What is this honor all about? It's about treating your parents with respect. It's about giving them a certain place of "weight" in your life—valuing them, respecting them, speaking well of them and thanking them for their place in your life.

I'm fully convinced that this commitment to "honoring" your parents can absolutely include and incorporate a drastic departure from "their way" of living out faith and involvement in church.

You may find that you prefer a different kind of music in worship, a different style of Bible teaching or a local church with a slightly different approach to doing gospel ministry. That's fine! Again, the biblical call for you is to give your parents honor . . . not imitation.

What do you think? When you're honest with yourself, how much have you tied Christian faith to your parents and their "experience" of Christianity and church? How much have you connected them to your view of Jesus and His body and grown cynical or disillusioned because of it? Part of the goal of this chapter is to confront you—perhaps in a fresh way—with the beauty of Jesus Christ and the necessity of His body, the church. I want to place that in front of you as prominent—the first issue that you need to deal with as an individual and independent adult. I will speak more on this in a moment.

The Church

Let me turn now, just for a few moments, to a brief discussion about the church. Many of you who may be reading this have grown cynical about the church; that's actually quite normal and common during the young adult years. But, before you dismiss the local church completely (or at least your involvement in it), let me just make sure we know what we're talking about.

The church is eternal, because God has
eternally committed Himself to its welfare.

Universal People, Local Manifestation

First, biblically, what is the church? Well, there are a few ways that we can think about the church in biblical language and concepts.

A People, Not a Place

Listen to these words from 1 Peter 2:4–5: "As you come to him, a living stone rejected by men but in the sight of God chosen and precious, you yourselves like living stones are being built up as a spiritual house, to be a holy priesthood, to offer spiritual sacrifices acceptable to God through Jesus

Christ." The church is not a place; the church is the *people* of God. Many churches have beautiful buildings and sanctuaries. But without the people of God gathering together, it would not be a church.

Something Jesus Loves

In the midst of Paul's teaching on marriage in Ephesians 5:25–27, we find remarkable insight on the relationship between Jesus and the church.

> Husbands, love your wives, as Christ loved the church and gave himself up for her, that he might sanctify her, having cleansed her by the washing of water with the word, so that he might present the church to himself in splendor, without spot or wrinkle or any such thing, that she might be holy and without blemish.

Jesus loves the church. Jesus died for the church. Jesus wants to one day present the church as forever holy and perfect. The church is something Jesus Christ—our Savior and Lord—loves dearly.

The Body of Christ

Ephesians 1:22 describes the church this way: "And he put all things under his feet and gave him as head over all things to the church, which is his body, the fullness of him who fills all in all."

Over and over again the Bible calls the church the body of Christ and identifies Jesus as the head. When you hear someone say, "I want to follow Jesus, but I don't want to be a part of a church," take the "body" imagery seriously and literally. When we attempt to follow Jesus apart from the church, we essentially tear apart the body of Jesus. We decapitate him. What may have seemed at first to be an almost righteous-sounding statement becomes fiercely sinful and disrespectful, and it flies in the face of everything the Bible tells us about the relationship between Jesus and His church.

God's Main Weapon in this World

We're too often distracted by the spots and wrinkles to see the great purpose and calling God has given to the church. Paul had a grand vision for the church when he wrote these inspired words in Ephesians 3:8–10.

> To me, though I am the very least of all the saints, this grace was given, to preach to the Gentiles the unsearchable riches of Christ, and to bring to light for everyone what is the plan of the mystery hidden for ages in God who created all things, so that through the church the manifold wisdom of God might now be made known to the rulers and authorities in the heavenly places.

Did you catch that final clause? God delivers his "manifold wisdom" through the church! He entrusts the greatest message in the world—the mystery of the gospel—to the church. There is no greater weapon God could have committed to His peoples' hands.

The Only Eternal Institution in the World

Of the world's many formidable institutions—governments, corporations, law firms and so on—only one will last forever. Listen to the apostle John's vision of the church—God's people—at the end of time, which he writes in Revelation 21:1–3.

> Then I saw a new heaven and a new earth, for the first heaven and the first earth had passed away, and the sea was no more. And I saw the holy city, new Jerusalem, coming down out of heaven from God, prepared as a bride adorned for her husband. And I heard a loud voice from the throne saying, "Behold, the dwelling place of God is with man. He will dwell with them, and they will be his people, and God himself will be with them as their God."

The church is eternal, because God has eternally committed Himself to its welfare.

Universal AND Local

We've been talking thus far about "the church"—meaning the "universal" church, comprising every believer in Jesus Christ who has ever lived. The "local" church has a more specific definition, but it does not belong to a completely different category than the universal church. The local church is a localized and organized manifestation of the universal church.

This means that everything we've been saying about the "church" can also, in general, be applied to the local church. We can't obey the Bible's instructions about life in the universal church unless we live them out in the context of a local church body.

As the universal church grew in the first century through conversions to Christ, local churches sprouted throughout the Roman world. This is why the New Testament usually calls a local church "*the* church at *x* city." It is THE church—localized in a particular way.

These local churches soon took on leadership and organization. Paul told Titus to "appoint elders in every town" (Titus 1:5) as a way to establish godly leadership at the various local churches and then gave him the spiritual qualifications for identifying these men. Local churches were characterized by two essential activities: the preaching of the Word and the celebration of the sacraments. Under these two core activities come other aspects of corporate worship: prayer, public Scripture reading, offering, singing and fellowship.

Observing this pattern, we understand the local church as a *localized manifestation of the universal church that meets regularly for the preaching of the Word and the celebration of the sacraments, under the leadership, direction and discipline of elders.*

Implications

Love for the "universal" church necessitates love for and commitment to the "local" church. So our local churches seek to manifest the universal church as a part of the body of Christ we can love, see, touch, struggle with, give to and serve.

Context for Faith

It's difficult to read and study the New Testament without coming to a very clear conclusion about the mindset of the apostles (Paul, Peter, James, John): They assume that the believers to whom they write are living out a personal faith in Jesus Christ in the context of the local church. It is their basic assumption that the church—the local body of believers—is the context for their faith. There is just no category in the New Testament for a "churchless" Christian. Everything in the New Testament is written to believers who are assumed to be in community with local believers in local churches.

Friend, if you do decide to be a Christ-follower, you're going to need the church. You're going to need a local body of believers to teach you, encourage you, challenge you and pray for you. You also need a church context in which to use your gifts to build up the body of Christ!

I'm going to end this chapter by telling you the opposite of this as well; not only do you need the church, but the church needs you!

You know that people can't actually be as "put together" as they seek to appear on Sunday mornings.

The True Gospel

If there is one final word, or call, I want to leave you with, it's quite simply this: If you're going to reject Jesus and His church, make sure that you're *actually* rejecting *Jesus* and His *church,* and not something else that has made you anger, bitter or cynical.

In other words, I want to challenge you to work hard to ensure that you know what you're turning away from. Look it in the face. Figure out what the Bible actually teaches. Consider who Jesus actually is. Find out what the local church is actually supposed to be doing. And, if you're going to walk away, walk away from the *real* thing.

My guess is that a lot of young adults have pictures and stereotypes (maybe even straw men) in their minds about Christianity and Christian churches. Over time, these pictures and stereotypes start to become the only reality they have when they think about Jesus and His people.

Sometimes, I think such young adults can be in danger of rejecting something that actually doesn't resemble closely at all the teaching of the Bible or the true community of faith that Jesus means to establish and lead.

Would you accept my challenge to look Christianity full in the face, and make sure you are walking away from the real thing and not a "straw man" you've created in your mind?

What You Reject

Let me take a stab at this. My guess is that if someone gave you this chapter to read, you've come to one or more (or maybe all) of the following conclusions about Christianity, Christian parents and the local church:

Closed-minded

As you've been exposed to more and more of the world and culture (maybe through going away for university or entering the workforce), you've become more and more convinced that Christians are incredibly closed-minded—resistant to new ideas or to honestly engaging with the opinions of those who disagree with them.

You've found Christians (perhaps even your own parents) to be stubborn, poor listeners and perhaps even unwilling to engage with anyone who holds a different viewpoint than they do.

As someone who has seen the value of conversation and engagement with different ideas, you simply hate this.

Judgmental

While you still hold a personal set of morals and a commitment to integrity (perhaps still even basically grounded in a commitment to God), you also have come to despise the mindset of many Christians who seem to impose their values on others and look down on "sinners" with spite, scorn, anger, disgust and even hatred.

Even when you disagree with someone's behavior, you work hard not to appear judgmental of that person; it makes you cringe the way some Christians talk about those engaged in lifestyles (or those holding opinions) that they believe to be contrary to Scripture.

Out of Touch

Even many of the Christians with whom you grew up and still love strike you as a bit "out of touch"—not really engaged with culture or the "real world" in the way that normal people are.

There are sweet and loving people in the church where you grew up, and you know that they genuinely love you and care about you (maybe even pray daily for you), but you also have a hard time getting over the way they simply seem to be caught in a different decade . . . or maybe even a different generation.

They sing hundred-year-old hymns, still go to church potlucks and don't know a thing about the world of politics or culture; many of them wouldn't last a day in "your" world. It's not that you dislike them; it's just that you would never want to be relegated to being that out of touch with reality, culture and the real world.

Fake

Everyone at your parents' church where you grew up still "dresses up" on Sundays for church. They sing the same songs. They plaster smiles on their faces. They greet each other with handshakes and trite phrases and small talk.

He invites you into sweet relationship with Him forever. Don't walk away from *Him*.

You hate this. You know that many of their families have serious issues. You know that people can't actually be as "put together" as they seek to appear on Sunday mornings in the worship service. It all just strikes you as fake. Disingenuous. You think to yourself: *Really?*

If church is a place for people who "have it all together," then it's not the place for you. And, it's not a place where you would ever want to bring anyone who has real needs, who is really messed up and is really seeking spiritual and emotional help. It's not that church services aren't "nice," in their own way; it's just that they don't seem authentic.

Holy Huddle

Here's the thing: It's not that the people in the churches you've been a part of are "bad" people per se. They're nice folks; they like each other; they've been kind to you. It's more that the whole church "thing" seems to you to be so turned inward—"curved" inward on itself, in a way. It's a "holy huddle"—a place where the Christians come together to have their safe place where they belong.

It's a clique that is focused on caring for itself, and not really concerned with looking outside of itself to the real problems and issues that plague our world today. Sure, your church is sending some missionaries to Africa and Latin America, but how are they engaging their city?

What are they doing to help young girls caught in prostitution or teenagers who are taken in by gangs, drugs and violence? How are they reaching out in love toward those who are caught in a homosexual lifestyle, rather than just "speaking out" against them from the pulpit?

You're turned off by a "holy huddle" mentality of church that doesn't seem to be looking outside of itself in genuine love and service.

Hypocritical

Maybe it was your pastor. Maybe it was a youth leader. Maybe a respected Christian coach, mentor, teacher or instructor. Someone let you down. Someone you respected as a man or woman of God (maybe even multiple people) had a serious moral failing and absolutely shattered your view of Christians and your ability to trust Christian leaders.

All of those years of teaching, witness, encouragement; all of those years of you looking up to that person as a Christian role model; all of those deep conversations where you opened up to him or her. It was all trash. Hypocrisy. He cheated on his wife and ran off with another women. She "came out" about the double life she'd been leading. He joined a cult and walked away from Christian faith. She had been stealing money for years in secret. He was addicted to child pornography. And you were done. Fed up. Finished with Christianity and Christians as anything more than hypocrisy and hypocrites. You won't be fooled like that again.

Again, maybe it's one of these issues. Maybe it's more than one—maybe all in some way—that have caused you to question the legitimacy of the church and the level at which you will give yourself to God's people in that context.

Let me be clear on something: All of those potential "issues" that you have with the local church are probably *real* issues, at least to some extent. Sadly, because churches are full of sinful people (as the whole world is as well), there are going to be messes, painful experiences and even shocking examples of sin and depravity.

Friends, you can and should reject these things. You should be disgusted by religious hypocrisy—people who claim to live for Jesus Christ and then secretly engage in behavior that is blatantly against His teaching.

You should be critical of a lack of authenticity in the church, which should be a gathering of people who are honest and open with each other about their struggles as they seek to live together for the glory of Jesus Christ.

You should despise judgmentalism, if it is unaccompanied by loving and gracious engagement with people who are in deep need of the healing and forgiveness that is found in Jesus Christ. I'm telling you that it's okay to be frustrated with things about the local church. It's even okay to reject some of those things, as you seek to help God's people grow, learn and be more and more Christ-like. But, there are some foundational truths and realities that I want to now call you not to reject, along with whatever issues you have with the church.

What You Shouldn't Reject

Friend, reject hypocrisy; expose it where it is found in the church, and call your peers and your brothers and sisters to live out genuine faith in Jesus Christ in public and in private.

Worship. Serve. Love. And let's grow
together to resemble our great
Savior more and more.

Reject a "turned inward" culture in the church, and encourage God's people to be "outward facing" with their faith, gospel witness and acts of mercy.

Reject judgmental attitudes, when they are not accompanied by a gracious invitation to find forgiveness and hope in Jesus Christ.

Reject a lack of authenticity on the part of sinful people who are struggling together to fight sin and reflect the Savior.

Reject a "holy huddle" mentality, as well as a church culture that prohibits a bold engagement with the ideas and theories of secular culture, for the sake of witness to Jesus Christ and His gospel.

But, friends, don't reject *Jesus*. He is the perfect and sinless Savior—the eternally existent Son of God who was active in the creation of the universe and the design of your body and soul. He loves you. He died for you. He rose from the dead. He reigns at the right hand of God. He will return to judge the earth and every human being who has ever lived. He paved the way to eternal life and peace with the God who made you, and He invites you into sweet relationship with Him forever. Don't walk away from *Him*.

And, don't reject the *true gospel*. Not other gospels; you can reject those. Reject the gospel of "good works," which would suggest that sinful human beings can earn their way into favor with God.

Reject the gospel of "entitlement," which makes privileged Christians less excited to share the gospel with marginalized and disenfranchised peoples.

But, don't reject the Gospel of the God who made you, who offered His Son in substitution for you, who deserved to be under His wrath and punishment for all eternity (see Eph. 2:1–3). Don't reject the good news that because Jesus rose from the dead, sins really can be forgiven and mortal humans really can have hope for immortality in and through the Savior. Don't turn away from that!

And, don't reject *God's people*. Yes, they're messed up. Yes, they're all recovering sinners who are saved by God's grace alone. Yes, they've got so much to learn, and the process of sanctification sometimes seems to take *so* long.

But, they're dear to Jesus. He shed His blood and gave His life for them. He's shown them grace, and you—as a brother or sister in the family of God—are called to show them grace as well. If you want to be in Jesus' family, you've got to get along with His kids; you've got to love the people He loves. Don't reject God's people.

And, don't reject the *local church*. Observe its failures. Note the ways it is marred by sin. Criticize it if you must. But don't leave it.

Don't abandon the local gathering of God's people. In short, do your work and make your critiques from *within* the body of Christ—a body of which you are a part of and to which you have committed yourself in membership, love and service.

Don't take off.

Don't reject the local gathering of God's people, for despite its weakness and warts and scars, the church is still God's plan for accomplishing His gospel purposes in the world.

A Final Call

We need you. Young adults, we need you in our churches. The local gatherings of Christians will be better for having you in their midst. Bring your concerns. Bring your issues. Bring your critiques. But join in. Identify yourselves with God's people, under the bright banner of the gospel of Jesus Christ, who is the only perfect One.

Worship. Serve. Love.

And let's grow together to resemble our great Savior more and more.

Notes

Chapter 1: Panic Attack

1. Jon Walker, "Family Life Council says it's time to bring family back to life," Southern Baptist Convention, June 12, 2002, http://www.sbcannualmeeting.net/sbc02/news-room/newspage.asp?ID=261.

2. Scott McConnell, "LifeWay Research Finds Reasons 18-to 22-Year-Olds Drop Out of Church," August 7, 2007, http://www.lifeway.com/Article/LifeWay-Research-finds-reasons-18-to-22-year-olds-drop-out-of-church.

3. "Most Twentysomethings Put Christianity on the Shelf Following Spiritually Active Teen Years," Barna Group, September 11, 2006, https://www.barna.org/barna-update/millennials/147-most-twentysome-things-put-christianity-on-the-shelf-following-spiritual-ly-active-teen-years#.V17AhrIrLIU.

Chapter 2: The Other Side of the Story

1. Jon Nielson, "Why Youth Stay in the Church When They Grow Up," *The Gospel Coalition*, July 29, 2011, https://www.thegospelcoalition.org/article/why-youth-stay-in-church-when-they-grow-up.

2. Rachel Held Evans, "Why Millennials Are Leaving the Church," *CNN Belief Blog*, July 27, 2013, http://religion.blogs.cnn.com/2013/07/27/why-millennials-are-leaving-the-church/?hpt=hp_c4.

3. "Bono's Thin Ecclesiology," *Christianity Today*, March 1, 2003, http://www.christianitytoday.com/ct/2003/march-web-only/29.37.html.

4. Jon Nielson, "Loving the Church" (message, College Church, Wheaton, IL, September 2014).

5. Ed Stetzer, "State of Church Planting," *The Exchange* (blog), Christianity Today, January 9, 2009, http://www.christianitytoday.com/edstetzer/2009/january/state-of-church-planting.html.

6. See www.thegospelcoalition.org and www.trg.org, respectively, accessed June 13, 2016.

Chapter 5: Principle 2

1. Jay Thomas, Personal interview with author, January 2015.

2. Tom Olson, Personal interview with author, January 2015.

Chapter 6: Principle 3

1. Personal interviews with author, February 2015.

2. Eric McKiddie, Personal interview with author, December 2014.

Chapter 7: Principle 4

1. Jon Nielson, "Family First in Youth Discipleship and Evangelism," *The Gospel Coalition*, August 11, 2011, https://www.thegospelcoalition.org/article/family-first-in-youth-discipleship-and-evangelism.

2. For a way forward on gospel-centered ministry, see D.A. Carson and Timothy J. Keller, *Gospel-Centered Youth Ministry: A Practical Guide* (Wheaton: Crossway), 15.

3. Jon Nielson, "Youth Ministry Done Well for the Benefit of the Church," *The Gospel Coalition*, August 18, 2011, https://www.thegospelcoalition.org/article/youth-ministry-done-well-for-the-benefit-of-the-church.

Chapter 9: A Way Forward

1. D.A. Carson, *Praying with Paul* (Grand Rapids, MI: Baker Academic, 2014).

Chapter 11: The Millennials and the Church

1. Larry Osborne, class notes, DMin course, Trinity Evangelical Divinity School, Deerfield, Illinois, 2014.

2. See www.billhybels.com and www.willowcreek.org, accessed June 13, 2016.

Chapter 12: To Those Who Are Mourning

1. Attributed to Ray Cortese, Senior Pastor, Seven Rivers Presbyterian Church, Lecanto, Florida.

2. Winston Churchill, "Never Give In" (speech, Harrow School, London, England, October 29, 1941).

PUBLICATIONS

Fort Washington, PA 19034

This book is published by CLC Publications, an outreach of CLC Ministries International. The purpose of CLC is to make evangelical Christian literature available to all nations so that people may come to faith and maturity in the Lord Jesus Christ. We hope this book has been life changing and has enriched your walk with God through the work of the Holy Spirit. If you would like to know more about CLC, we invite you to visit our website:
www.clcusa.org

To know more about the remarkable story of the founding of CLC International we encourage you to read

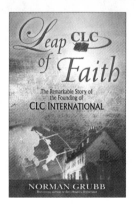

LEAP OF FAITH

Norman Grubb
Paperback
Size 5$\frac{1}{4}$ x 8, Pages 248
ISBN: 978-0-87508-650-7
ISBN (*e-book*): 978-1-61958-055-8

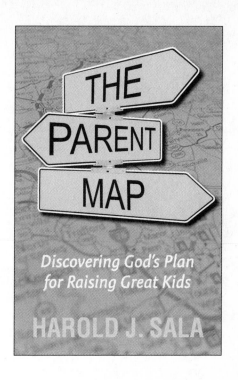

THE PARENT MAP

Harold J. Sala

Harold J. Sala, author of over twenty books on marriage, presents a new book that focuses on equipping parents to raise godly children in the face of today's unique cultural and social challenges. In straightforward language, Sala examines different parenting styles, focusing on both the mother and father's role in the parenting process.

Paperback
Size 5¹/₄ x 8, Pages 274
ISBN: 978-1-61958-217-0
ISBN (*e-book*): 978-1-61958-218-7